Accolades for Companioning the Sacred Journey

"JoAnn's book has become like a good friend--gentle, clear and profoundly wise. If you are on a spiritual path, this book is a wonderful and true companion."
~Denise Rushing, Author, Tending the Soul's Garden

"This very sweet, touching and practical writing...may very well be the beginning of your journey to living your life's purpose. At the very least, your heart will be touched and it's simple, yet heartfelt process, may change your life..." ~Vicki Crystal, Intuitive Life Coach

"JoAnn's book spoke to me and touched my heart giving me the tools I needed, when I needed them, to deal with a difficult period in my life. I know her heartfelt stories and guidance will serve me well in the future... This is a book that should be included in anyone's library, to be taken as a companion as they travel on their own personal journey." ~Judy M.

"JoAnn's telling of her very personal journey is inspiring, motivational and practical. Even if you are not on a spiritual path, but are curious what the excitement is all about, this book may be just what you need to start on the road of personal discovery, happiness, and fulfillment. And who doesn't want that?!" ~James A.

D1601716

Companioning the Sacred Journey: A Guide to Creating a Compassionate Container for Your Spiritual Practice

By

JoAnn Saccato, MA
aka Awakened Presence of the Heart

Companioning the Sacred Journey: A Guide to Creating a Compassionate Container for Your Spiritual Practice

Shylila Lassie Moon Publishing
P.O. Box 1332
Cobb, CA 95426

Cover art and design by Kathy Wolden, www.kathywolden.com
Photo of JoAnn Saccato by Glo Photography/Gloria Salvante

www.companioningthesacredjourney.com
P.O. Box 1332
Cobb, CA 95426

To receive a free gift for purchasing this book, visit:
http://www.companioningthesacredjourney.com/receive-your-free-gift.html

ISBN-13: 978-0615874951 (Shylila Lassie Moon Publishing)
ISBN-10:0615874959

Dedication

I bow in deep gratitude and dedication to my many teachers on the sacred journey: H.H. Dalai Lama, Jack Kornfield, Ramana Maharshi, Neem Karoli Baba, Thich Nat Han, S.N. Goenka, Walter Robinson, and so many more. But most deeply, to my long time companion and teacher on the sacred and secular path, Shyla (aka Shylila Lassie Moon).

Gratitude

This book would not have been possible without the support, artistic vision and guidance of Denise Rushing, Kathy Wolden, Sandy Lenhardt, Loretta McCarthy and Gloria Salvante. It also wouldn't have been possible without the loving support, feedback and encouragement of my intimate partner, Jim Leonardis.

It is only by sitting at the feet of the Bodhisattva of Compassion that I have been able to complete this work. For that I bow the deepest.

Table of Contents

Preface

The oaks are almost bare. The remaining leaves dangle in the fall wind, dry and crackly. Shyla pauses and stillness takes over. I follow her lead, as I'd done literally thousands of times throughout the ten years we'd spent living remotely at the cabin. She scans the canyon laid out before us. Every time we come down the hill, she does this. She does it with the time and attention one would either use the first time seeing the view, or possibly knowing it would be the last.

This was her last. Not that we knew it then, but we knew it.

We were making a final trip up the hill to clean the cabin and retrieve some remaining belongings--mainly, a couple of solid wood and green leather dining chairs found free alongside the road during our second year living there. We wheelbarrowed those and other miscellaneous items that we needed for our next adventure together--our new home on Cobb Mountain.

As Shyla descends the glorified deer trail, she is unable to move her hind legs in full range--a sign of her age. Instead, she leads with her front legs and her back ones kind of hop to catch up. It's hard to tell if she's in pain, but since they can't move fully, I assume she is experiencing some discomfort at the very least.

Up the next slope she pauses again, this time by the overlook to our benefactor's monument. I reflect on our friend Walter who had offered us the cabin as a home when the end of a 13-year relationship found us homeless. The Tibetan prayer flags flap gently in the breeze and a wooden striker twists and turns, tenderly tinkling the long metal rods on an aging set of chimes. Shyla again scans the scenery.

Over the years, Shyla's growing consciousness continued to amaze and inspire me. As we had settled into the cabin and our voluntarily simplistic lifestyle, her presence and awareness grew to like that of a seasoned monk--intentional, in the moment and bright.

Our relationship with Walter was one of spiritual companions on the path. While he had passed a few years before, connecting with him was as easy as pausing momentarily and bringing him to mind. Voila! His consciousness was with us and sometimes Shyla would react as if he were there--with a skittish concern and distancing that reflected her relationship with him while alive.

We spent many mornings and late afternoons at his monument space. An oak tree's low reaching arms stretched above and around the stone-cast Buddha statue placed in his memory by his family. His ashes tucked close behind in a simple plastic container with various colorful silk scarves draped over it, a sacred space was created. The usual altar accoutrements-- candles, incense and vases--are further behind, protected from the elements by the muscular oak.

A lit candle, some billowing incense, an offering of fruit and one of Shyla's biscuits in the offering bowl was our usual alms at this site which was the site where Walter camped some 30 years prior. It was fitting that this be his final resting place. He so loved the land--this land where he lived with family and ultimately in solitude until his final year.

I would sit and meditate facing out towards the canyon, aside the Buddha, and Shyla would put her back to me looking up the hill, as was common when we were outside together. She would usually take a view that could oversee everything, and, if she could, she would tuck herself into a spot where she was protected from behind. She was always on alert when we were outside together. Her Shepherd nature, I thought.

Always protective and aware of my whereabouts, whether I was cutting and gathering wood, sitting and meditating, practicing Xi Gong, or eating, Shyla was my companion--spiritual, physical, emotional.

One morning in meditation, about a month after she had passed, I saw Shyla's life in metaphor. A petal in the blooming flower of life. A soul in the awakening consciousness. Still part of the whole awakening, but an individual petal that grows and falls of its own accord, living within the limits of the laws of nature.

My life too, of course. I am but one petal on the flower of awakening. The importance in playing my role in the blossoming is to be as present with the whole process as I can. As well, to bloom and be part of the bigger blossom in the most magnificent way I can.

It is also to accept the eventual aging and dying of not only other petals, but inevitably, myself. My intention is to do this gracefully.

Shyla is a petal that has blossomed and fallen gracefully for me and before me...She not only gave me the gift of her life in companionship, but I also had the gift of her death, literally in my arms, as conscious and incredulous as all that can be.

In the Buddhist tradition, the Buddha, or the One Who Knows, is the One who not only experiences the whole blossoming process through each of us, but observes it as well. It is the awareness that witnesses the All That Is.

In this quote by Rumi:

> *The truth was a mirror in the hands of God. It fell, and broke into pieces. Everybody took a piece of it, and they looked at it and thought they had the truth.*

I think this is so true. By holding up a piece of the mirror to ourselves, we do see the truth--but only a part of it. We are that mirror of God. We are God. But only a part, a piece, a petal. Vitally important to the blossom and vitally true, but only with all the other petals in any given moment do we become the totality of God.

This book, this teaching, is but one petal in a flower of information, insights, stories and pictures on awareness, self-transformation and sacred spiritual journey. And, as with most flowers unfolding, the essence and fullness of the unfolding remains to be seen.

How will this petal in the flower of life affect you?

As I once shared with Walter: One purpose of existence is to directly experience the unfolding. Upon further reflection, another is to be touched by the experiences of others in their blossoming and to allow that touch to affect us and our choices. We are all interconnected. We cannot NOT be touched by what is happening around us. Our openness to this determines the depth with which we can blossom in our own lives--with which we can contribute to the whole blossom of existence.

It is with kind regards, that I hope that you, the reader, be touched in some positive way by the stories and teachings contained in this book, and may it bring some benefit to you in your awakening--in your own sacred journey.

I

Companioning the Sacred Journey

Companioning the sacred journey is for those of us who are looking for a more authentic, deep and meaningful experience in life. It is for those of us undertaking a conscious spiritual path--a journey of the sacred. We'll learn to discover and accept the companionship of our loved ones, traditions, community and even the unexpected. Most importantly, though, we'll learn to companion ourselves on this journey and discover what a good companion could do and can be for us as we reach for a deeper and more meaningful life.

Companioning the Sacred Journey is about learning to create what I call a *compassionate container* for our journey--about putting together the pieces and practices that create a safe, beautiful and durable space and attitude for our voyage.

It is about learning to become free enough of our thought processes to choose compassion and aliveness within ourselves and on our journey. It is to learn to stay present with ourselves even when we are blocked, scared, angry, or otherwise acting without conscious intention.

Together, we'll learn practices that will help us do this for ourselves, our loved ones and the larger community. We'll discover that our companions can be the unlikely--the stickery neighbor or aloof co-worker, the four-legged friends we care for, or the children in our lives.

Mostly, we'll learn to be present on our path, to consciously set intention, learn how to forgive ourselves even when we can't be present and to compassionately show up again and again for our process of discovery--our life.

Companioning the sacred journey is about being willing to show up for it all--the good, the bad, and the ugly--the breathtakingly awesome journey that is life. It is about learning a set of tools that opens our awareness and directs our experience to living our lives as fully as possible. You've taken a step to this life by picking up this book--opening yourself to the possibility of a wakeful aliveness and presence in your sacred journey. For that I acknowledge and honor you!

We'll begin our journey together with looking at how we can companion ourselves with the very foundation of a sacred journey--a self inquiry. We'll use mindfulness meditation as the foundation of a spiritual practice and guided reflections at the end of each section to help further the exploration. We will also explore companions in others, companionship for others, and companioning our community.

This will be a journey of self- and other-discovery that has the potential to transform your life and relationships to a deeper, more fulfilling and authentic way of being.

II

A Compassionate Cautionary Note

"Reading is at the threshold of the spiritual life. It can introduce us to it; it does not constitute it." ~ Marcel Proust

I would be remiss as a teacher, companion and a student on the path if I didn't give this kind warning. For those of us that have or are suffering from mental disorders; post-traumatic stress disorder (PTSD); previous or current physical, psychological, emotional, or financial abuse; and/or a current or past addiction, please take note. Undertaking a path to self-awareness and authentic living may trigger and bring these issues to the forefront. This is actually a good thing--if we have the proper tools and support to help us navigate wisely through the necessary healing.

My intention is to help you by guiding you to a set of tools to better deal with these conditions, if they exist. By creating a compassionate container for the deep healing work that may become apparent as we shed the layers of conditioning, we are better able to heal these past or current traumas.

I am not a therapist or a doctor of psychology. My expertise and offerings are based on my direct experience, those of my friends on the path, the teachers I've worked with, the books I've read and the different healing modalities I've either experienced or practiced.

If I become aware that a client of mine has one of these conditions, and I sense difficulty arising, I will most likely ask them to work concurrently with a professional as a condition for our working together.

If you have any of the conditions I described above or discover them as we journey together, I wholeheartedly encourage you to seek out professional help and guidance. The wisdom of adding this "tool" to help maintain a safe container for your inquiry is the most compassionate and loving thing you can do for yourself and your healing journey.

III

Companioning for Self

Journaling as Companion

There is nothing more important in a journal than the capturing itself.

I begin with journaling because it is a way to take note of our experiences, explore our emotional self and companion our sacred journey. You may find it useful to use a journal as you read this book for the guided reflections at the end of each section. As well, the discovery of our thoughts and feelings through journaling can be a cathartic process that opens the way to our emotional self and healing. It is a process that bares witness to our experience and becomes a trusted companion for that experience, for it will not reflect anything other than what we put into it and it will not judge us.

My first journals began in middle school as exercises in writing class and consisted of binder paper, a pencil and direction from my teacher to just write about what I was thinking. At that rebellious, unconscious time in my life, entries were mainly about how dumb school was and, in particularly, the writing exercise at hand.

In college my journals consisted of spiral notebooks and were mainly about activities and feelings. It was then that the cathartic process began to take hold. My journal became a tool to work through personal issues; where I could talk with someone who would see my situation without judgement (even though I was full of usually disdainful judgement toward myself and others).

My journal was the trusted friend that could understand my reasoning and logic (or illogic, as the case was at times), my humor, my desires and passions, my heartbreaks and triumphs. From there, my journals became a life companion. They recorded dreams, the song in my head when I awoke, impressions of life, my relationships and excursions. I spent more time with my journal and began paying more attention to their style, finding actual blank journals with attractive covers and paper.

My early journals are lost, but I accept this as a shedding of an old self. I was painfully stuck in a loop of emotional torture, like that of being stuck in a whirlpool--unable to swim hard enough against the drowning current to get free. They reflected the pain and suffering of a young woman reaching out to find the deep answers to life--looking for an end to the painful suffering that arose from being raised in a family with addiction and violence issues, as well as the adopted patterns of my own addictions and codependence. They voiced the cries of my not knowing how to live or who to be, the hopes and dreams of finding fulfillment and being rescued from a life of bane existence with little depth or meaning, except when delving into life's deep questions.

I have a friend who throws her journals away when they are filled. It is a freeing process for her, because she sees herself as ever growing and changing. This is somewhat like the Tibetan tradition of creating and destroying sand mandalas to demonstrate their temporariness.

The cathartic process aside, my journals also reflect a growth and process of discovery that I hold very dear. They are a priceless and powerful companion on my path.

If you have not journaled before, the invitation is to find a medium that will inspire you. Some prefer paper and pen/cil, others appreciate the efficiency of the computer. Still others use tossed out paper and write in all the white spaces.

If at first the process seems awkward, consider you are writing to a dear, trusted friend that you can divulge anything and everything to and you will be understood, not judged, and truly cared for. If you are of a faith, you might consider your journaling a conversation with the deity of your religion or the Universal Intelligence.

Here are a few guided exercises to consider for your journey and the first of the guided reflections in the book:

Guided Reflections

 Upon waking, record your dreams and any impressions you have about the dreams. Note if you feel refreshed or tired and how your state of mind is. Do this for a few weeks and then look back from the beginning. What do you notice?

Before bed, write a summary of activity for your day as well as your emotional impression and reactions of your activities. Also, make note of three things that you were grateful for that day.

 Sitting in your favorite spot, write a description of what surrounds you. Have you co-created this spot, or is it untouched nature? What is it that inspires you about this spot? Why is it your favorite?

As you develop your intuitive self through these exercises, your dreams, impressions, and states of being will begin to align more closely with each other. You'll be able to gain more insights through journaling.

I remember when I was traveling in Mexico many years ago. A friend had won a trip for two and I had only happened to go because his romantic interest at the time wasn't available to travel. It was a last minute, unplanned trip for me.

We took a bus tour in Mexico City which included a stop at a famous Catholic cathedral. As we entered with the tour guide, I was stopped dead in my tracks. I had been there before! It wasn't that I had seen this cathedral--either on TV or in a brochure (this was before the internet)--but I had actually stood in the space before.

As we walked on, I was reliving a scene I knew well that included a massively large picture of the Mother Mary hanging on a wall. Visitors could walk down in front of this image while passing to the lower level of the cathedral and view the massive portrait from just beneath it. The floors were concrete throughout and Mass was held hourly, 24-hours a day.

At this particular time, the floors were being washed and water was running down the concrete walkway that went underneath the picture of Mary to the lower level. As we walked down, there were vendors selling trinkets and treasures to the visitors.

Where had I had seen this before? I had lived this! Even to the minutest detail like the wet floors! Incredulous, I couldn't figure it out and was deeply troubled by it--I was experiencing déjà vu.

Upon return to the States, I flipped through my journal of the time and sure enough almost six months prior, I had had a dream of this place and captured it with the detail of the presence of the wet floors. In the dream, though, I had jumped up on a concrete platform to stay dry and chat with a lover.

Incidents like these helped propel me forward on the spiritual journey and deepened my respect for my dream life and my journal. The songs I would wake up with in my head in the morning would begin to reflect my frame of mind and emotional state. These tools became a powerful companion to my eventual healing and life.

Mindfulness Meditation as Companion

> *"It [mindfulness] is an exploration of how the mind works and how it can be stilled so as to reveal an inner spaciousness in which wisdom and compassion arise with ease." ~David Richo, How to Be an Adult in Relationships*

> *"Mindfulness is a method of exploring what it is to be human." ~Sandy Boucher*

Mindfulness is a process by which we become actively aware of our direct experience. Through a series of ever deepening periods of awareness--meditation sessions--we become intensely aware of our experience in the moment. We can benefit greatly through this process just as it is, sitting on our cushion, but the real magic is how the practice affects the rest of our life--without our explicit effort.

We work on training the mind to become acutely aware of this moment's experience by learning to focus our attention on our senses. Amazingly, those same five senses we learned about in primary school can be used to profoundly affect change in our lives.

By giving a kind and curious attention to our direct experience, we weave the beginnings of a compassionate container. Every emotion such as love, sorrow, joy or anger is available to us only in the present moment--truly, it is the one place we can experience them. As many of my teachers have put it, love in the past is but a memory and love in the future is only a fantasy. Paying attention to this moment gives us the opportunity to experience all of our life fully.

By shifting our focus and releasing ourselves from the need to control and create our experience to one of just becoming present in the moment through our senses, we can discover that our experiences include profound instances of joy, awe-inspiring gratitude, deep sorrow, fiery anger and sometimes tremendous fear.

While our culture encourages us to spend billions of dollars annually to protect ourselves from the unpleasant emotions and billions more to give us (if only temporary) the pleasant ones, the effort to create or not create particular experiences is actually part of the cause of our continued suffering.

Interestingly, though, we will not be able to enjoy the full expanse of the positive experiences unless we also open fully to experience the perceived negative ones. What I have discovered through years of pain, suffering and finally releasing the need to control my emotions is that unpleasant emotions are nothing to fear. Quite the contrary. When experienced fully, these emotions are as life-giving and fulfilling as some of the most positive ones. Some of my most profoundly enriching life experiences were during the most dramatic losses of loved ones and periods of deep despair.

Through mindfulness meditation I've learned that no state of being exists forever and that our comforts and discomforts are temporary and always changing. Meditation is now coming to the forefront of being seen as healthy and beneficial to our mind and body. I invite you to investigate the possibility of this discovery for yourself by exploring the following mindfulness exercises. In the short run, you may experience a welcomed period of relaxation, peace and calm. Over an extended period of time, consistent practice will reveal a steady groundedness and an ever deepening pleasant wakefulness outside of practice.

If you approach mindfulness meditation with the combination of effort and an openness to grace, as author David Richo invites, then I assure you, you will open a profound chapter in your life. This ethic of a balance between concerted effort and a letting go of expected outcomes also translates to a valuable guiding principle for life itself. It is also the same formula that allows grace to reveal itself.

Guided Reflections

 What is your initial sense of mindfulness meditation?

How to Begin: The Beautiful Container

Creating a beautiful and pleasing physical space for your practice helps create a sacred container where you can consciously practice with kindness, attention and awareness.

The invitation is to create a physical space that is as free of distractions as possible, is inviting and pleasing to you and where you can enjoy a period of time that is undisturbed by interruptions such as telephones or people walking through. You will want this space to include a place where you can sit comfortably either in a chair or with cushions on the floor.

Take some time to make this space special for you. You might place some meaningful objects close to where you will be sitting. You can build a little altar that has a photo or three dimensional image depicting someone or something you respect, maybe a deity from a religion you are drawn to or a teacher that you admire.

Over time, as your practice continues and your intuition grows, this space will evolve to include other objects that become sacred and valuable to you which may include candles, incense, objects from nature (rocks, leaves, flowers, water, etc.). Allow this space to evolve with your practice, keeping it fresh for you--sometimes being simple, still and quiet and other times busy and colorful. What is important is that it has meaning for you.

For myself, the condition of the space makes sense for the time and I build a ritual around attending to it and the altar. There are times when I desire simple elegance, which, for me, conjures a sense of timelessness and stability. Other times, my altar will fill up with objects that have come to me or attracted me, which reflects the abundance of experience, relationship and internal objects in my life.

When the time is right, usually when a staleness or clutter seems to settle into the area, a ritualistic cleaning will help sweep through the dust and debris, revealing a whole new altar and shifting the energy in the space. There is always a sense of "ahhhhh" and freshness for me when this happens. I also notice this shift in the rest of my life when a cleaning takes place on my altar.

Give yourself room to play with this sacred container you are creating and know that there is no right or wrong about it--only how it feels to you and supports your practice.

Guided reflections

 What do you notice over time about your sacred space? Does it help create a sense of sturdiness for your container? Whimsy and play? What is the texture it brings to the container?

How to Begin: Posture

Include in your sacred space a chair or cushions where you can sit comfortably for a period of time. If you choose a chair, choose one where your feet can touch the floor or use a cushion so your feet can rest comfortably with your legs uncrossed. If you choose a cushion, be sure to have several smaller supporting cushions at your fingertips that can be used to keep your spine straight, but not rigid. These cushions may be propped under your knees, to ease tension in the back and legs; on your lap, to release the tension in the shoulders and upper back; or to add height under your buttocks.

Zafus are traditional meditation cushions and come in many styles and colors and are stuffed with different materials. There are numerous sources for zafus on the internet. You can also use household cushions. The importance is your ability to sit for a period of time comfortably.

If you sit on a chair, a simple straight backed chair can help facilitate a straight spine. While some use the back of the chair to support their back, others sit on the edge of the chair so that the back is unsupported, as if you were sitting on a cushion.

If you sit on a cushion, you'll want to find a way to sit so that your hips are above your knees. For beginners, this can mean using extra cushions for height and support under the knees until the muscles stretch into the desired position. Some yoga postures can help facilitate the body's ability to sit on cushions for periods of time. One of my teachers shared that the purpose of yoga was to prepare our bodies and mind to sit for meditation. The important thing in the beginning is to be kind and gentle with your body and use any additional supports needed until the body opens on its own, which it will do over time with continued practice.

You may also want to experiment with a meditation bench which allows for the knees to tuck under the bench where you sit. Evaluate to see which works best for your body and over time you will develop your own style and comfort.

I have experimented with round and crescent zafus and have settled with a crescent shaped one which facilitates my feet and knees the best. When I'm on retreat and we sit multiple times daily, I mix up my sitting postures to relieve the stiffness that inevitably comes from long periods of time in the same position. I turn my crescent on its side and sit up on my knees, placing the cushion under my buttocks as if I were using a meditation bench.

Remember to be kind and tender with yourself as you explore sitting positions. Cultivating equanimity while sitting in excruciating pain is a lot tougher than beginning slowly in comfort. And, while some traditional practices encourage this, I have found that in the beginning, adjusting my sitting as needed to maintain a relative state of ease was the most beneficial for my practice.

How to Begin: This Breath, This Moment

"Mindfulness is a Buddhist-inspired concept that emphasizes active attention on the moment to keep the mind in the present." ~ Julie Watson

"Sitting quietly with our eyes closed for even as little as ten or fifteen minutes a day begins to 'clear the waste' out of our hearts and minds, making room for the nourishment of peace and wisdom to enter in. To sit in meditation is to tune your ear to the voice of the Sage, and it is the most powerful way of gaining his assistance." ~Brian Browne Walker, The I Ching or Book of Changes

Mindfulness is simply cultivating our awareness of our direct experience in this ever-unfolding present moment. We practice mindfulness by returning our attention again and again to the present moment regardless of how often our attention has wandered away.

For myself, after many attempts of trying to "meditate," resulting in only a few seconds of sitting still and lots of self-recrimination and disappointment, I realized I needed guidance. I attended a 10-day silent meditation retreat in Southern California founded by a world renowned Burmese teacher, S. N. Goenka.

Our training started with the breath as the object of focus for the simple reasons that the breath is with us all the time, it takes no effort on our part to generate it and it is constantly changing and in motion. Focusing on the breath frees and retrains that part of the mind that is used to directing and controlling things and repurposes it to accept and observe the direct experience through the senses.

There are many different styles of meditation. Attention and focus are directed in different ways depending on the lineage, teacher, temperament of the student, etc. Each of these practices has incredible value and have proven over time to create wakefulness, enlightenment and profundity. (If you are interested in a comprehensive compendium of styles of meditation in Theraveda Buddhism, see Jack Kornfield's Living Dharma: Teachings and Meditation Instructions from Twelve Theravada Masters.)

I enjoy working with the breath as the object of focus because it is varied and alive from moment to moment. It is always changing, with me wherever I go, and always present. My mind wants to control it when it becomes the focal point, so with every breath comes the opportunity for awakening to a more authentic experience through letting go of the need to control.

You may wish to use the breath or any other object that you can continue to refocus your attention on during meditation. Some are attracted to candle flames, a photo of a deity, or a mantra (a repeated sound, word or phrase). Each has their benefit but for simplicity's sake, and reasons that will become more apparent later, I will use the breath as our focal point.

Simple Breath Meditation

Once you have settled into your seat, take a look around the room. Take a moment to notice the colors, textures, shapes and lighting of the objects around you. It is only in this moment that these things are in this particular configuration. Bring a curious attention to the details you see.

After a few moments, close your eyes and begin to focus on the sounds you hear. Allow them to seep into your awareness and notice if they are loud or soft. Are they ongoing? Sporadic? Sharp? Dull? Again, using a curious attention, discover what is presenting itself in this moment.

Notice if there are any fragrances present. Can you smell anything? If so, with a kind, interested observation, what do you notice? Is the fragrance strong? Sweet? Pungent? Pleasing? Offensive? Dense? Light?

Bring this growing mindful attention into your mouth. Can you taste anything? If so, what is the nature of the flavor? What is the texture? Is it dry? Wet? Sour? Pleasing?

Now, move your attention to your body. First, take notice of the major sensations you feel most. Maybe you feel the pressure of your buttocks on the cushion or chair. Maybe it's where your hands are resting. Just allow your attention to notice the most pronounced sensations and if there is any discomfort, use this time to shift and adjust as necessary to make yourself even more comfortable.

Scanning through the body, lay your attention to rest in the area where you most feel your breath. Maybe this is in the belly as it expands and contracts. Or maybe you sense it most in the chest. Perhaps it is the opening of the nostrils as the air moves in and out. Just allow your attention to settle on the area where you most sense it.

Bringing that same kind, curious attention that you used with your senses, what can you discover about the breath as it happens in each moment? Is it rapid? Slow? Smooth? Erratic? Consistent? Deep? Shallow? What about the texture? Does it feel humid? Dry? Is it different on the inhale than it is on the exhale? How does it change over time?

Without trying to change the breath, take about 15 minutes to explore its nature as it presents itself in each moment. If you notice your mind has wandered, just gently bring your attention back to the breath in this moment. Shift and adjust your body as necessary to stay comfortable and continue to resettle your awareness back to the breath.

If you noticed your mind wandering during this brief, simple exercise, consider yourself part of the human race--the nature of the mind, as you discovered, is to think--just as the nature of the nose is to smell, the eyes to see and the mouth to taste.

As we begin this path, we may find ourselves somewhat shocked and dismayed to see this nature. Rest assured, you are not alone if your mind wandered a hundred or even a thousand times in that first 15 minutes of meditation! (As you may have noticed, the mind seems to have a mind of its own!)

The training we are undertaking is to bring the mind's focus to the direct experience of this moment. Our task is cut out for us! While the instructions are simple, it is not always easy. And for some of us, it is rarely easy--especially in the beginning.

I'm here to encourage you to not lose heart! Begin to see the practice as that--a practice of returning our attention again and again to this moment.

Guided Reflections

 How many times do you think your mind wandered during the breath awareness exercise? Were you surprised?

After meditation, briefly jot down your experience for that session including any major sensations, emotions, or thoughts and your reaction to them. After a while, read back over your journal. What do you notice over time?

How to Begin: Experienced Sense in the Body

Listen to the sacredness of this moment.

The Buddhist teachers I have worked with have all insisted that I not take their word for the truth, but actually discover directly, for myself, this truth. While I may share mine and others' experiences on the path, my invitation to you is the same--see for yourself. What do YOU discover? This is truly the key to companioning yourself on this journey.

After a period of time of breath awareness meditation, as described above, when you have refined your attention and your mind is getting used to refocusing on the present, you are invited to gently open up your meditation practice to include the experienced sensations in the body.

In some traditions, this can be the practice of a recurring, methodical scanning of the body from head to toe and back again. By beginning at the crown of the head, the attention is focused on the physical sensation present on the surface of the skin. Inch by inch, the attention is moved to the next area of the skin until a sensation is felt. This continues all down the front and up the back of the body on a continuous cycle until a bell rings, signifying the end of the meditation.

It can also be a more spontaneous practice of allowing your attention to go to the area in the body where the most pressing sensation is felt. Sometimes, the practice is a combination of both of these techniques--bringing the attention to minute sections of the skin then to broad expanses of the body.

In any form, the intention is to expand our awareness that we have just refined to include physical sensations. Our penetrating awareness is now used to focusing on the body so that our direct sensations of this moment are at the forefront of our experience.

As you work with your sensations, bring that same kind attention and curiosity that you did to the breath. Especially when working with the strong sensations that can be considered painful, a compassionate inquiry and kind attention is how we can best companion ourselves through this process.

Meditation on Sensation

After getting comfortable for your meditation, take about five minutes to settle into your breath. Once your attention is focused on the breath, bring your awareness to the area above your upper lip where the breath enters the nose. Allow your attention to focus on this patch of skin and explore the sensations you experience as the breath goes in and out.

Notice the temperature, texture, speed and depth of the sensations on the upper lip. Do this for 10 or so minutes. Then bring your attention to the top of your head and begin to slowly move your awareness to a spot below the crown in a section of about two inches square. Wait until you feel a sensation, then move adjacent to this spot to the next two-inch square. Repeat this back and forth slow sweeping down the front side of your body.

When you have reached your toes, begin the same process up the back side of your body until you reach your crown. Continue this sweeping up and down the body. In the beginning, take your time and discover every nook and cranny of your body and every sensation. A full sweeping will take about ten minutes.

In general, you are continuing to sweep at a steady rate. After a time, though, if you notice there are areas of sensation that are more pronounced than others, take a few extra moments in these areas to discover a few things: 1) Where does the sensation begin and end? 2) Is the sensation permanent or fleeting? and 3) What is the nature of the sensation--dense, tingly, solid, sharp or pleasant?

At the end of your sitting period, take a few moments and do large sweeps down the front of your body and up the back.

Sensations are critical for experiencing our lives authentically and fully and for moving us into more mindful living--where we consciously choose our path. As we move into working with our emotions in our meditation, sensations become even more important as they are inextricably connected to each other.

An alternative method is to allow your attention to follow the most noticeable sensation in any given moment as it arises in the body. This creates another opportunity to let go of control and experience what is in each moment.

Guided Reflections

 What did you notice about the sensations in the exercise above?

 Over time with this practice, what do you discover about your body? About sensations in general?

Emotions as Companion

"Do not let another day go by where your dedication to other people's opinions is greater than your dedication to your own emotions!"
~Steve Maraboli, Life, the Truth, and Being Free

"I'd want them to know that their experience is part of their humanity, part of the difficulty and the gift of human incarnation and we are all called upon to bear our sorrows as well as our joys, and that we can bear them and they're not the end of the story."
~Jack Kornfield in an interview with Elisha Goldstein

Emotions are a gateway to the very depths of our experience as humans. Some of us, though, have learned how to set aside our emotions. Some of us were raised in families where any sign of tears were met with "buck up" and we were told to "quit your crying." This seemingly harmless approach to emotions can teach us a valuable skill--setting an emotion aside--but my experience has seen that rather than to set something aside temporarily, it is used to stifle these emotions permanently, which is harmful to our bodies and our psyche and teaches us to not trust our emotions, and thus ourselves.

This can make it difficult to navigate our lives for our highest and best good, as our emotions can be an invaluable guide to making important decisions. This practice of stuffing our emotions can also result in a patterned, rote response to life. It can mean we have to stay on guard to our emotional state and control or ignore our natural responses, rather than assess them and respond considerately.

Our mindfulness practices can help us unlock these stifled emotions. It begins with learning to experience our emotions fully in our body and then deciding how to respond to these emotions in a way that will foster healing and growth, courage and conviction, and/or release and mourning.

A good companion knows when it is important to take the time to dive deeply into a situation, set it aside temporarily, or let it go completely. Much like a kind parent who knows us the deepest, learning to distinguish the appropriate response to our emotions at any given moment is a learned art, but it can only be practiced when we are fully in touch with our emotions.

When we begin exploring our emotional states in our practice, we may discover emotions that have been stored for many, many years. We may become in touch with and overwhelmed by emotions we never have felt fully--even those from when we were quite young. For some of us, this can mean a lifetime of emotions that have not been experienced, acknowledged, attended to, cared for, or released.

They may seem huge and overpowering, and for a time, they may be just that, because we may have spent most of our life "setting them aside." These emotions and feelings end up being stored in the body. This is why our practice of experiencing sensations fully becomes critical to our practice and a very important part of our compassionate container for our sacred journey.

Opening up to our emotions creates an incredibly powerful opportunity for healing and release of blocked energy in our bodies and in our lives. The invitation is to become really present with the process through experiencing the physical sensations that arise during our practice and in our day to day life. For it is in these sensations that emotions play out.

In my childhood, I was taught that certain emotions were okay to express, but others were not. In the unpredictable and chaotic upbringing of abusive alcoholism in my family, there was never a consistent message regarding the expression of emotions. For my own safety, this led to a life of learning to control my every expression. I learned to walk on eggshells around my family.

It was also the way I thought I had to be around everyone else and I resorted to using drugs, alcohol and tobacco to suppress and "manage my feelings." Unfortunately, this manifested in a pattern of a chaotic cycles of suppression and rebellion through uncontrollable outbursts.

I first started experimenting with feeling my emotions in adulthood directly after I quit drinking and smoking pot, only to find that tobacco was the last tool I used to stuff my feelings. When I finally let tobacco go, there was nothing to keep me from experiencing my feelings. At this point on my spiritual path, I was ready to release all barriers to this direct experience as I knew from teachings, readings and others' stories that I couldn't heal and get emotionally well without a deep acquaintance with the full gamut of my emotions.

I distinctly remember when I undertook the inquiry of discovering what all the fuss was about with emotions. Why shouldn't I feel these feelings? Are they so intense of an experience that they could harm me? I set myself down on the dry hillside just outside my cabin early one January morning. I allowed the intense emotions that were arising from an incident in my current relationship to express themselves without trying to hold them back.

I had worked enough with mindfulness to know that the goal was to sit with whatever arises and to focus my attention on the physical sensation. I was scared because of what I had been led to believe about emotions--they would literally consume me.

The waves of sensation arising were powerful. I kept breathing and doing all I could to not stifle or direct the energy that began to course through my body. Instead, I kept opening to receive it fully. Tingly, but spacious pressures came and went--sometimes dense pressures, sometimes open and loose--but it was a constantly changing form of expression that moved through my body.

Tears fell and crying lurched forth from deep within my heart and lung space. I couldn't name or know what I was feeling, but it felt so wonderful to feel it without trying to constrain or control it. It was a release that opened my lungs to beyond full capacity and felt deeply healing and really, quite pleasant. Not pleasant as in joy, but opening, effortless and liberating! A freedom like that felt when holding onto a steering wheel too long and hard and finally letting go. Deep sighs and release followed.

What was all the fuss about? Why didn't people want me to feel certain feelings? Why was so much energy expended to stop this process--both from individuals and from society at large? And why did I adopt this suppression over time when my own experience showed me something different?

During this initial phase of feeling my feelings, tears became such a cleansing release of tension in my body that even today I do nothing to hold them back. I see them as just part of the whole experience of life and to me they serve a deeply valuable function in determining my actions and path.

What I mainly recognized through this journey, though, was that people didn't want me to feel or express certain emotions not because they were harmful to me, but rather because my emotions and reactions evoked certain reactions in them that were uncomfortable. Today, my emotions along with the sensations in my body serve as an invaluable companion and serve as an important compass in my life. They are the window to my intuition and indicator for making decisions.

Through stifling my emotions I was able to do things and witness things that my conscience would never have allowed. I can see there is a value to this ability when used for self-discipline purposes, but what I really see is the impact on a culture that has allowed this stifling to permeate the social body so deeply, that we have lost touch with our conscience in so many ways.

Our emotions point to a truth that is arising. When we cry in fear or pain, we are witnesses responding to what is happening around us. For me, this was the witnessing of the abuses inflicted by an angry and drunk father. In this experience, it was not only not okay to feel, but it also wasn't okay to speak about what went on.

Some 40 years of stifled emotions were pent up when I made the commitment to feel my feelings. I had no idea that each and every one of them was still stored in my body and would rise to the surface for release after layers of conditioning were liberated. When I first started this practice, I wondered if the rest of my life wouldn't be spent in overwhelming emotional overload such that I began to wonder if the accusations of my parents were true--that I was "too emotional."

As the healing work continued and I worked directly with the emotions and the physical sensations, the initial intensity subsided. On occasion, another layer of the onion would peel away and I would discover another treasure to release. Now, though, I mostly experience and express my emotions as they arise, without fear or shame. They move through the body effortlessly and I usually experience a not unpleasant release.

There are those occasions when strong emotions arise and it may not be the appropriate place or time to look at and experience them fully in that moment. Because I have done this deep work and created a safe and compassionate container for my experience, I can set aside those emotions temporarily, knowing that I have built into each day the time and space for my practice where I can explore them more fully.

Companioning ourselves includes the capacity to experience and be present with the gamut of emotions that are such a vital part of being human. Just as we would want to be there for our good friend or our own child, we can create a compassionate response for ourselves. For some of us this is a learned practice, for others it is as natural as breathing.

Now that your attention has been refined further through the practice of focusing and observing the breath and bodily sensations, the ability to experience your emotions in your practice is available to you. The invitation now is to expand your mindfulness practice to include your emotional life, allowing time to experience directly in the body the physical sensations that arise as a result of emotional states of being.

Take note of the emotional vibrations and sensations as they move through you and what you are feeling.

If you are new to feeling your feelings, I encourage you to find a list of common emotional states. These helped me over time to learn to discover and articulate what I was feeling.

Guided Reflections

 Keep your journal with you and periodically throughout the day jot down any emotional states that you notice. Include the situation that occurred when the emotions arose. In a few weeks, read back over your entries. What do you notice?

 Take note of how you respond to people that are experiencing a particularly difficult emotion. What are the sensations in your body? What is your reaction?

Weathering the Storm

In the living room in my new home, there is a window that is situated across from the couch where I sit for meditation. It is literally a picture window, as the scene is something you would see in a magazine: the long, thick trunk of a large pine tree with a deeply grooved texture, scattered maple leaves and pine needles, all resting on the top of an old rock wall. Ivy and Vinca are spilling about the place. It is very picturesque and a pleasing sight.

When I meditate in the morning, it is sometimes before daylight, though by the time I finish the soft morning light brings to life this picture of serene, majestic beauty. At other times, it is already light when I begin meditating and I am engrossed and captured by the beauty.

On one particular morning after Shyla's death, when I had still only been living there a few months, it was daylight and had started to snow. (This made me giddy, as I love the snow!) The birds darted in and out of view of the window, scratching and pecking around for seeds and bugs. I couldn't help but open my eyes on occasion during meditation to see what was happening next.

The precipitation turned from rain to snow, again and again. Sometimes the wind picked up and the snow would come across the view almost sideways. Other times, I would see the Stellar Jays bully their way with the smaller birds and each other.

In this moment, I was so happy. The smile on my face was as wide as it had been since Shyla passed. The giddiness was bubbling up from deep inside and a profound sense of gratitude washed over me. My goodness was I grateful! I thought to myself, "Thank you! Thank you for this moment, no matter how long it lasts!"

I closed my eyes and within a short period of time the thoughts around whether or not I was going to get to stay in my home, which was involved in a convoluted foreclosure scenario, crept up again. It was quite uncertain what the outcome would be. Taking note of these thoughts and refocusing back into the body and breath and sensation, I settled back in.

My eyes opened again to a different scene outside: the sun partially shining through, creating a glistening yellow tint to the tiny patches of snow that had stuck, causing a twinkling reflection off the ivy.

Slowly I realized that the window frame was capturing what was passing before it and just allowing it to happen. It hadn't anything to do with what was happening, it was just allowing it to be seen. It wasn't reaching out toward it. It wasn't reacting to it. It was just allowing it to pass before it, much like the calm clear awareness does when the mind is settled and quiet.

When we are practicing mindfulness, actively observing our thoughts, they arise and pass, just as the birds darted in and out of this scene. The weather changes much like the thoughts in the mind do: the snow gets intense and blustery or the sun shines stark clarity. As well, the mind can be busy and bustling or calm and clear and everywhere in between.

My pure awareness is witness to all the thoughts and changes without interaction, disturbance, or attempts to change it. It just receives it as it passes through. Sometimes, like the steady solid tree in the scene out the picture window, a thought pattern or a particular situation in life will remain for a very long time, and other times, like the fleeting weather or the bird, it will dart in and out of our mind or life in an instant.

Sometimes what arises in our mind's eye is ugly and painful to watch, like the bullying by the Stellar Jays, and sometimes it's stunning beyond comprehension, like the majestic awesomeness of redwoods swaying in a strong wind.

When the stillness in our being is nurtured and we are not actively seeking and reaching out towards something or pushing away from something else, our experience can become one like the picture window. We just relax unattached and enjoy the show that passes our way. We become less entangled and caught-up in the wanting and not wanting of a particular situation or outcome. It is then that we become still enough to receive the gifts of the arising and passing of nature--our own and others. This is what is referred to as equanimity. In equanimity, there is less pain and suffering and more joy and bliss because there is less wanting and not-wanting--less grasping or pushing away of any particular experience.

When we use mindfulness as our companion, our capacity to become like the picture window grows and we are more open to receive the grace and bliss that arises naturally in events. We are also better able to weather the storms of life, because we can rest in the surety that these, too, will pass.

On this particular morning, I was able to see that the path to purchase my home was like riding on a bumpy dirt road on a bad stormy night. There were lots of bumps and swerving, it was hard to see where I was going and I didn't know when or if I would get there. I could better remain calm now, knowing that, like the changing scenes in the picture window, I could just be present with wherever I was on this road and know that it would most likely change.

Regardless of the outcome, whether I ended up staying in this home or not, I could provide a compassionate container for myself during this home buying experience and not be too attached to each swerve and curve in the road. With practice, I can weather all the storms of my life as they arise. I can do so lovingly with kind attention and a curiosity like that I bring to my meditation practice.

Guided Reflections

 Are you weathering any storms in your life right now? If so, what type of compassionate container can you create for yourself for the process? What could help you soften the ups and downs of the journey?

 If you are in a difficult period, bring this to your cushion with the intention of observing it through a clear window. Watch as the events and your reactions have changed. See if you can take on the perspective of a compassionate observer that doesn't know the outcome, but, like hearing the story from a friend, has a genuine concern for their wellbeing.

To the Edge and Soften

"Most of us do not take these situations as teachings. We automatically hate them. We run like crazy. We use all kinds of ways to escape -- all addictions stem from this moment when we meet our edge and we just can't stand it. We feel we have to soften it, pad it with something, and we become addicted to whatever it is that seems to ease the pain." ~ Pema Chodron, When Things Fall Apart: heartfelt Advice for Hard Times

Seemingly contradictory to Pema's quote above, Tibetan teacher Chögyam Trungpa taught that the essence of liberation was to meet our edge and soften--only with our mindfulness and compassion, rather than an external substance. This practice allows the inevitable "edges" of life to be met, mindfully, without running.

This practice can help create a little more openness and opportunity for co-creation with trying circumstances. It can teach us how to create a more spacious approach when things are tense and rigid. If even a little more spaciousness can be brought to a situation, then our choices can expand and we are less likely to react in a way that is harmful for us or others.

In your practice, this can easily be explored by sitting in a position a little bit longer than is comfortable; reaching the edge of comfort and consciously meeting that edge head on and using our kind attention and compassion to soften it.

If you are experiencing a particularly trying time in your life right now, or have chronic pain, try working this meditation practice into your daily routine.

Edge/Soften Meditation

After settling into your meditation, when you begin to notice discomfort in the body, allow your refined attention to focus directly where you feel the pain. With the same kind and curious attention you have brought to the other meditation exercises, can you pinpoint where the pain begins and ends? What are the sensations associated with it? Are they sharp and stabbing? Dull and achy? Throbbing or steady?

Spend a brief time exploring this with your clear, sharp, focused attention. Then, shift and expand your focus to include the immediately surrounding area that is not in pain. Open up a bit further and include a larger area that is not in pain. What do you notice about the painful area from these new perspectives?

After a bit of time, bring your focused attention back to the painful area. What do you notice now? See if you can consciously relax the area a bit. Maybe a deep, cleansing breath shifts it. If so, what happens?

After a time exploring like this, shift your position to one that is comfortable. Bring your focused attention back to the area that was in pain. What do you notice now? What sensations are present?

We can take this edge/softening practice into any realm of our practice (physical, emotional, thoughts, etc.) and our lives. Actively participating in our experience in a mindful and compassionate way can empower us in many ways, provide a freeing and expansive approach to difficult situations and many more options to our life choices.

In Motion

"The whole point of classical yoga as described in Patanjali's Yoga Sutras-the basis of modern yoga-was to prepare the body and mind for seated meditation." ~Yoga Journal

"Mindfulness is our ability to be aware of what is going on both inside us and around us. It is the continuous awareness of our bodies, emotions, and thoughts." ~Thich Nhat Hanh

"Qigong is the meditative art of conscious embodiment. It recognizes, honors, cultivates and nourishes the 'energy' aspect of our being. Qigong perfectly complements traditional sitting meditation practice and has a long and well-established history connected to contemplative traditions. It is, in fact, a complete meditation practice in itself." ~Teja Bell

You may have noticed by now with your sitting that there are very few moments of actual stillness. As well, your body may become stiff after extended periods of sitting or parts may actually fall asleep. Except for my initial retreat, which emphasized the letting go of all physical exercise routines for the duration of the retreat period, most practices I've explored have encouraged physical motion and bringing mindful attention to the body in motion.

Everything from walking meditation to yoga and Qigong, finding one or many complementary mindful moving practices is supportive to the awakening in the body, the resting of the mind and the integration of sacredness into our daily lives.

Many of the ancient body movement practices and martial arts are centered on working with the life force energy of the body. In Sanskrit, the language of the origins of yoga, this is called *prana*. In the ancient orient, *chi* or *qi* was the term used for this vital energy and is used today in healing practices such as Reiki.

As for building our sacred container, if the essence of the practice you choose is one of mindfulness--cultivating awareness of this energy and movement--then it will be supportive of your practice and journey.

I find myself doing more yoga in the active months, spring and summer, and notice a tendency in the fall and winter to want to work with the more subtle energy movement forms like Qigong, and Tai Chi, where less action is supportive of connecting with the energetic forces more easily.

Each of these movement practices support my sitting practice in differing ways and a sitting practice helps bring more awareness to movement practices. Together, they both support bringing more awareness and aliveness to all activities in life as we are more able to integrate focused awareness into daily activities.

Amazingly, something as mundane as washing dishes became one of the first areas that I moved mindfulness into my daily life. When I lived at the cabin, dish washing could sometimes take an hour or so from beginning to end. I heated the wash water either on the wood stove or the propane stovetop. Because I had a limited source of water, I managed my resources frugally and used only two-and-a-half gallons of rain water to wash and rinse a sink full of dishes. This lent itself to a mindful practice in needing to attend to every drop of water. But, I also found it very moving, as a lot of our lives are spent in ongoing chores like doing dishes and laundry.

Dancing can be another form of movement meditation. Traditional forms such as Sufi and shamanistic dancing and experimental forms such as Trance Dancing offer many opportunities for mindful exploration. I led a weekly dance workshop called TranscenDance! which began by creating a safe place for everyone to explore their body. Then, through varying musical genres from around the world, we would free-form dance for about 45 minutes. These forms of movement can be freeing to the mind and body, leading to a more authentic experience for the dancer.

You may want to explore a particular practice for multiple sessions to find the ones that work best for you. For myself, it took many sessions to discover some of the energetic benefits of these practices, as well as move through barriers that sometimes presented themselves as a result of conditioning.

The important thing I found was to find practices that created a shift of energy that was enlivening to me both on and off the cushion. For some, this may be a slow moving guided practice to calm the frenetic mind, for others, it could be a frenetic freeing form that releases pent up tension in the body. After a while of practice, you'll begin to know which form will support your particular mind/body state at any given time and you'll offer yourself these practices out of kindness for yourself.

Guided Reflections

 Do you have a mindful moving practice? If so, what are the benefits that you've noticed?

 If you don't, which practices attract you? Spend some time on the internet exploring these further and reach out to find a class or gathering to attend.

Affirmations

"Act is the blossom of thought; and joy and suffering are its fruits; thus does a man garner in the sweet and bitter fruitage of his own husbandry."
~James Allen, As a Man Thinketh

"Your thoughts and beliefs of the past have created this moment, and all the moments up to this moment. What you are now choosing to believe and think and say will create the next moment and the next day and the next month and the next year."
~Louise Hay, You Can Heal Your Life

Affirmations are just gratitude in advance for that which you are intending to create. They are a declaration of truth; the intentional use of carefully crafted statements that are repeated over and over with the intent of having them become the truth. They can be spoken out loud, internally to oneself and/or written down. They have been seen as a path to miracle cures and miracle manifestations, as well as general statements of intention for one's life.

I was first introduced to affirmations in the early '80s when a coworker, Linda, was diagnosed with breast cancer. The New Age movement was taking hold at that time and I was busy exploring what it had to offer.

While we weren't very close, my co-worker Linda introduced me to Louise Hay's work, *You Can Heal Your Life,* which dives wholeheartedly into affirmations and their healing potential in every aspect of life. In Linda's personal journey, with the help of this book, she was able to trace some deep resentments to over-mothering her brother and eventually came to believe that she was carrying these resentments in her breasts as cancer. Although Linda eventually passed from her disease, she was able to die a peaceful death having done some deep-rooted emotional healing work with herself and her brother.

As a result of my exposure to Linda's process and Louise Hay's work, affirmations became one of the first tools I took up to reprogram my inner mind talk from one of self-hatred, anger and resentment, to one of love, abundance and worthiness. To this day, I use affirmations to help clarify my intentions and manifest my life.

For an affirmation to be most effective, it is best that it be composed in the present tense, be positively oriented, have very personal meaning and be either a generalized statement or very specific, depending on the desire. Affirmations are very powerful when practiced with genuine sincerity. They are closely related to visualizations, which is mentally painting a picture of a scene down to the minutest detail.

When my father was dying in the early '00s, I was making many trips back and forth to Oregon to his business. My long-term relationship was dissolving, though I didn't know it, but I knew deep down I was not living life to my fullest capacity-- and I was caught in unhealthy and dysfunctional lifestyle choices.

On one particular trip, Shyla and I had to camp for a couple weeks while we closed my father's business and auctioned off his assets. It was a stressful time, as my father was still alive, recovering from a stroke. He had to come to grips with the dissolution of his business. There was familial discord between other siblings, myself and my father surrounding the choices being made with his properties.

Knowing I was going to be there for a while, I went into a used bookstore in the small town where I was staying and looked for something inspirational and meaningful to tide me over for the journey. There, perched in the New Age section was a previously loved copy of *You Can Heal Your Life*. It had been fifteen years since I was introduced to the book and I found myself drawn to it like an old friend.

The book begins with learning to understand our issues and their source and then moves into how to recreate the life we want to live by focusing on a particular area of life, including our health, prosperity, relationships and more. As I worked my way through the book, I started memorizing the affirmations that were at the end of each chapter. Each chapter's affirmations begins with, "In the infinity of life where I am, all is perfect, whole and complete," and ends with, "All is well in my world." I learned the paragraph-long affirmations until I could recite them by heart and did so diligently every day. It took me about a half of an hour and it was the perfect thing to do while driving to work, as it set my consciousness in a place of openness, healing and clear intention each day.

Within a matter of months from beginning this work, my whole life fell apart, but I remained optimistic--because I wasn't living a life I wanted anyway. I continued diligently with my affirmations, even when everything around me didn't look like what I had in mind. It turned out that the dissolution of everything in my world was necessary so my life could recreate itself in a new way.

I began adopting thoughts and ideals for the life I wanted to live and focused on releasing the things that no longer served me. I wanted a deep and meaningful spiritually-based and emotionally mature life filled with prosperity, loving relationships, purpose and travel to different cultures. In addition to reciting the affirmations I found in Louise Hay's work, I took the knowledge I learned about affirmations and started crafting very specific, well thought out statements to create this new life. And it worked--far beyond what I had ever hoped for!

This powerful practice of thought creating reality was addressed much earlier in the classic, *As a Man Thinketh*, by James Allen in 1902. Allen, an obvious pioneer of the self-help movement, was a philosophical writer and poet in England. He believed that thought coupled with purpose become a creative force.

Around the same time, French psychologist and pharmacist, Emile Coué, was considered the father of applied conditioning. In his work with hypnosis, he focused on the Law of Concentrated Attention which states that whenever attention is concentrated on an idea over and over again, it spontaneously tends to realize itself.

In my personal quest for understanding the underlying principles and truths of the universe, I researched quantum physics, because this was the science of the smallest known particles to our scientific community to date. I wanted to find out what was true all the way up and all the way down. I read physicist Fritjof Capra's work, *The Tao of Physics,* which helped me understand these underlying principles and dynamics.

Scientists have discovered that at the quantum level, there is no real solidity to any particle, nor is there any guaranteed performance or outcome of anything. There are only high probabilities that things will act a particular way, but they are only probabilities--even if extremely strong. During their research, scientists also stumbled upon the fact that the observers of the experiments seemed to influence the end result of the experiments based on their expectations of the outcomes. In other words, their expectations affected the outcome of the experiments.

To me, this was the answer to how we create our own reality. If things only have a tendency (no guarantee) to act a particular way, then there is room for influencing that tendency and hence the outcome. This is where there is room for "miracles" to reveal themselves.

When I lived in the cabin, I created a "Let God (the Tao, the Source, the Universal Intelligence, etc.) Do It!" pile for my affirmations. This is where I place the affirmations that I am working on for myself and others. I regularly reference and read these affirmations as part of my weekly routine.

When a situation eventually came to fruition, the slip of paper would then be placed in the "God Did It and I'm So Grateful!" pile. (But, really, these piles are one and the same because knowing that once the word is released into the universe, it is only a matter of time, attention and intention before the manifestation appears in the physical.) There is a constant flow in and out of each of these piles. Sometimes, the affirmations stay for long periods of time, like general desires for non-harming or surrendering to the divine unfolding, as these may take many years for me to gain competency. Others zip in and zip out, like my latest automobile acquisition.

When I remember that I have the creationary power of the universe on my side, my thoughts come from a space of gratitude, which is then reflected in my affirmations. They usually begin with, "Thank you that..." or "I am grateful that...", because what I have come to realize through my study and work with affirmations is that they are extremely effective. I can confidently begin from the place of knowing it has already occurred. They are in the works on an energetic level once I begin the conscious effort of intention and attention, and it is only a matter of time for them to come to fruition in the physical world.

Because of the power of thoughts, wording is of the utmost importance when putting directed attention towards creation. Designing affirmations is a practice in precision and clarity, with an openness to flexibility and revision.

I've found that if I am specific enough in my affirmations about what I'm wanting, but not so specific that it narrows the opportunities to very few, or works so much against the tendencies of nature, something magnificent will eventually manifest. For example, when it was time for Shyla and I to move off the hill, my affirmation became:

> *"Thank you! I have the perfect-for-me living space.*
> *I am in a wonderful place! It fulfills all my needs*
> *and desires. It is in a beautiful location and at a*
> *price I can easily and comfortably afford."*

The Universal Intelligence was able to know what a "perfect-for-me" living space was and what I considered beautiful--even better than I was able to envision! I was eventually moved to a home that was far grander than I had in mind. This may stem from one of my ongoing affirmations:

"God, the Source, the Tao, the All That Is has in store for me far grander ideas and experiences than my mind or body could ever comprehend, much less create. I lovingly, gently and effortlessly surrender to the unfolding of this eternal moment."

When Shyla's declining health became apparent, I wasn't sure I would be able to provide the best care for her, but I wanted to, desperately! My affirmation became:

"Thank you for my good friend, Shyla. Thank you for guiding me in how best to care for and love her as she finds her way to You."

As time went on, I did know what to do for her best care. I believed in my affirmation and then focused my time on being present with her and in my body so that I could better receive the guidance I was asking for. That is one of the biggest roles we play in co-creation--to cultivate the fullest presence in this moment as we can.

My "God did it and I'm so grateful!" pile is overflowing with affirmations such as these, as well as tickets to places i've traveled, pictures of people I know or have known, my graduation notices, and then some. When I look back at this pile and all the beautiful and amazing experiences I've had as a result of my journey on the spiritual path and affirmations, I am truly and deeply humbled.

We are more powerful than we know. If we can turn that power toward creating meaningful experiences for ourselves, we will know no bounds and our lives will become a reflection of this beautiful creationary power we all possess.

There are many resources for affirmations online and in books. I work with my clients through an inquiry practice and then help them carefully word their affirmations to best reflect their deepest desires. I also put my energy towards their affirmations, as the more thought power focused on the same vision, the quicker and more likely it will manifest. Sharing your affirmations with friends, who you trust will want your highest and best good, will multiply the power of this process. You can always start with generalized affirmations for yourself and others, such as:

"I am so grateful that I am open and experience my highest good and truth. I'm so grateful I've released the patterns in my consciousness, mind and body that keep me from living this highest good and truth."

Also, I've found that I have revised affirmations as my process unfolds so they better reflect my deepest understanding and desire. For example, if my affirmation started out as wanting a particular model car, I may come to realize that really what I want is a car that will provide for me particular services and comforts. With Shyla and myself, I wanted a car that we could take on traveling adventures, so my affirmation became:

"I love myself, therefore I provide for myself a comfortable car. One that fills all my needs and is a pleasure to be in. It is dependable, reliable,

environmentally friendly, and meets all of mine and Shyla's needs for our traveling adventures."

We only need to listen to our inner thoughts and look at our outer world to know how powerful and effective our thoughts can be. With this in mind, as you begin your work with affirmations, make a concerted effort to keep your thoughts focused, pure, compassionate and kind towards yourself and others.

Also, as you begin to say things from a positive perspective of what you would like to create in your life, pay particular attention to your mind's reaction and response to the affirmation. Sometimes, resistance or disbelief is an indicator that we may first need to let something go before we can replace it with something better. Willingness to release these thoughts, patterns and external circumstances that no longer serve us may be the first step in our work with affirmations. Keeping that in mind, here are a few ideas to get you started.

Guided Reflections

 Are there things in your life you would like to release or create? If so, with a thoughtful reflection, can you bring yourself to believe that they could possibly manifest for you?

 Pick one area of life you would like to see a change in. Take some time and visualize and journal what the ideal scenario would look like. Write as many details as you can. Then, write an affirmation for that scenario. Feel free to find other resources of affirmations to help you. Repeat the affirmation as many times a day as you can for the next 30 days. Reflect in your journal on the process during this time, as well as the result at the end of the 30 days. For big changes, you may only notice the shifting and changing towards something, or the releasing of what you no longer want. Continue the affirmations and revise as you discover these shifts and changes.

Affirmations are potent. Like any of the practices discussed in this book, working with them becomes a lifelong practice to be developed slowly, compassionately and thoughtfully. In working with affirmations I wish for you what a friend recently wished for me on my house search, which works as a wonderful catch all affirmation:

"May you be extremely happy with the outcome!"

Song as Companion

"If I'm going to sing like someone else, then I don't need to sing at all." ~Billie Holiday

"When we die, we will turn into songs, and we will hear each other and remember each other." ~Rob Sheffield

For as long as I can remember, I almost always awake with a song in my head. When I was quite small, I used to joyously sing a little ditty:

Sweet dream's a day
All in a row
A day

The song made perfect sense to me then and I loved singing it and other songs. It wasn't until I read Wayne Dyer's translation of Row, Row, Row Your Boat that I realized how true my little song was. Each day is a sweet dream and they are just piled up one after another.

I have exquisite early memories of joy and happiness. Today, when I am with very young children, I get to see that same joyful nature and can again touch it in myself. It is a sweet reminder that when the layers of conditioning are peeled away, or have yet to be layered on, a vibrant and playful self is naturally present.

I saw this in Shyla, too. My sense is that dogs, in general, are naturally resilient and don't hold on to states of being. Shyla was a great teacher on how to let things go and live in the moment. She had a sweet playful nature that stayed with her throughout life. Even after her ability to run and jump was hindered by age, I could still see it in her and it touched me and gave me a sense of playful joy.

I think that's why I believe that joy is our true nature. Because even as the body ages and passes away, that buoyancy and enthusiasm that we experienced as children still resides inside us, even if it can't be physically expressed as wildly as in our youth.

Guided Reflections

 What was your favorite song as a very young child? What did it mean to you? When did you sing it? When did it go away?

From where does song arise? I never set out to "write" the little ditty above. It is something that arose when I was in a state of freedom--a very small child that had yet been indoctrinated away from my inner self and awareness.

It is kind of like the process with Shyla's name. Over time, she took on numerous names that seemed to fit her personality and the stage in her life:

> *Shyla*
> *Shylila Lassie*
> *Shylila Lassie Moon*
> *Shy-ma*
> *Shy-shy-ma*
> *Ma-shi-pa*
> *Mashima*
> *Mash-a-ma*
> *Pa-shi-ma*
> *Pau-pau*
> *Paup-e-ma*

These names reflect a continual emergence of who she was and what was happening for her over time--all the way until her elder wisdom stage at the end of her life. We shed her names like she shed her coat, which she did virtually year-round as she was a Shepherd-Akita mix. Her development, temperament and personality evolved and blossomed and her names reflected that growth. It was a playful process that emerged naturally with us.

I have also heard of a tribe in Africa, the Ubuntu, that has a sweet practice with song. When a woman discovers that she is carrying child, she and the other women of her tribe go out into nature. There, they pray and meditate until the song of the child arises. This becomes the song that is sung throughout the child's life, from its birth through all significant events.

It is told that if a child becomes errant or gets into trouble, the tribe will sit the child in the center of a community circle and they will all sing the child's song to help the child remember who they are.

Guided Reflections

 Do you have a song?

 What songs attract you? Are they light, airy, loving? Do they bring a heaviness or darkness to your day?

 What happens over time with your musical tastes and your relationship with music as your journey on the path continues?

The beauty of our journey is that we can cultivate differing states of being through that which we expose ourselves. I invite you to pay attention to the songs that attract you. Take notice in your body how you feel when different songs are being played. What is the direct sensation felt? Is it pleasant? Unpleasant?

As we begin to awaken and peel off the conditioning of our lives, a lightness and playfulness can arise much like when we were very young. Some of us are fortunate to have been able to carry this with us into adulthood. When we learn to companion ourselves, the joy and playfulness that is part of our true nature can surface, or resurface. Discovering or rediscovering this playful nature and fostering it through song is a empowerment process. (I continue to sing my little dream ditty as a gentle reminder of how to live today--that this day is the destination.)

Explore what types of music give you a pleasant sense of lightness and allow yourself the joy of hearing this music to uplift you and use it to cultivate joyous pleasure. After many years of not listening to popular music or music with lyrics, when I was exposed to them again, I could see that my state of being and mindfulness was impacted most immediately and strongly by them. Because music so influences our state of being, it's important to choose the music we listen to wisely.

I can also see how the songs of my youth shaped my thinking while growing up. I have to pay close attention to what I am programming my very susceptible mind with. Am I filling it with "poor me" songs? "Love gone wrong" songs? As my sensitivity grows, my tastes in music changes and I am sure that when I do listen to music, that it is uplifting for my mind, spirit and body.

The Sacredness of This Oh So Brief Moment

"There is a brief moment when all there is in a man's mind and soul and spirit is reflected through his eyes, his hands, his attitude. This is the moment to record." ~Yousuf Karsh

"The Breeze at dawn has secrets to tell you. Don't go back to sleep." ~ Rumi

Buddhist teachings are grounded in the basic principles of no-self and temporariness. The concept of no-self is a challenging one to grasp from within our bodies and mind, but when we consider it closely, it is easy to see the truism.

You may have noticed with your meditation practices, as you sat with yourself, that you were able to see there was no final state of being. Your experience was always in flux--whether it was from the breath moving the body or the mind busily wandering away. If we look at life a bit closer, we see that it, too, is a process--something that begins with a birth, is constantly changing, and ends with death. Rather than a finished product, we can see that there is no solidity or final "object" in ourselves. This experience and knowing makes the thought of temporariness and no-self a bit easier to grasp.

This can be very disturbing and a conundrum to the ego, though! Bhagavan Sri Ramana Maharshi, a spiritual master from India, based his teachings solely on the self inquiry of "Who am I?" as an attempt of tracing the ego back to its source.

A sage once asked where the flame goes when one extinguishes a candle. As a student on the path, I found this a difficult question. Where did it go? The sage answered plainly that it is gone. Period. The fuel of the flame, in this case the wax, is still there, and unless the wax was completely burned away, it can still be re-lit. Where did the flame come from? It was lit by something else.

These questions can relate to human life as well. From a human perspective, some spark ignites a process that seems to begin in the womb and ends, if we're fortunate, when the body has been all used up. Keep this in mind for a moment.

My meditation ritual includes burning an incense stick. It not only serves as a time keeper, but the fragrance aids in keeping my attention on the present moment, as well other beneficial responses to the mind and body from the aromatherapy aspect of the fragrance. (For instance, some fragrances like lavender create a relaxed but alert body and mind.)

One morning, I could smell a stark change in fragrance as the incense burned down into the ash bowl. During that time, I was reminded how life winds down, and of Shyla in particular. Where did she go? The end of her life, like the change in fragrance as the stick reached the ash, was a stark difference to the joyful and rich expression of Shyla's life.

When the stick had fully extinguished, the fragrance lingered in the air for quite some time, which I likened to my experience with Shyla. My experience of her essence comes and goes, like an incense fragrance weaving in and out of space. Sometimes the nose of my heart can catch a whiff of her, sometimes it eludes me.

Those brief moments that are captured with her spirit enveloping me are the sweetest moments I know. And they are brief and not often enough!

I can't answer where the flame goes, or what happens when we die, but these questions do reinforce for me that we are here only temporarily and it is only in this moment that we can experience our lives. Only this moment to taste, touch, smell, see and hear all that is present for us. It is the only moment that we can experience love. It is a moment that is constantly changing and slipping away while another one is approaching.

This moment becomes sacred because of these very facts. If I try to hold onto it--whatever "it" is: Shyla, a feeling, a memory, an experience--it will elude me like the vapors of an incense stick or a butterfly being actively pursued. But, if I sit still, present, in this moment, with grace, the fragrance, like life, will awash over me and bathe my senses with the sacred sweetness of its essence.

Awakening is like this. If pursued, the pursuit will push it away. If present and alert in this moment, with grace, we will be touched by it--if only momentarily.

Recognizing the nature of being--that it is a process unfolding, much like the life of a flower--brings an immediate sacredness to the moment. This amalgam of conditions and circumstances that creates this moment will never, ever occur again. It can only be experienced once--now. If we aren't awake and present to experience this moment as it occurs, we will never experience this moment. It will be gone.

Through our cultivation of awareness and our commitment to the sacred unfolding, we increase our ability to experience the graceful and deep and meaningful experiences that make up our life.

Guided Reflections

 Has there been an instance in your life where you touched that place of knowing that there is only this moment? What were the circumstances? What did you notice in your senses?

 If you haven't experienced this before, take a moment right now to look around you, presence in your body and ask yourself whether this moment, with everything as it is, will ever occur again? What do you think about that? How does that feel--what is the felt sense in the body?

Source as Companion

"The best teachers are those who show you where to look, but don't tell you what to see." ~Alexandra K. Trenfor

"The tao that can be told
is not the eternal Tao
The name that can be named
is not the eternal Name.

The unnamable is the eternally real.
Naming is the origin
of all particular things.

Free from desire, you realize the mystery.
Caught in desire, you see only the manifestations.

Yet mystery and manifestations
arise from the same source.
This source is called darkness.

Darkness within darkness.
The gateway to all understanding." ~Lao Tsu, Tao Te Ching

"The most beautiful thing we can experience is the mysterious. It is the source of all true art and science. He to whom the emotion is a stranger, who can no longer pause to wonder and stand wrapped in awe, is as good as dead—his eyes are closed.

The insight into the mystery of life, coupled though it be with fear, has also given rise to religion. To know what is impenetrable to us really exists, manifesting itself as the highest wisdom and the most radiant beauty, which our dull faculties can comprehend only in their most primitive forms—this knowledge, this feeling is at the center of true religiousness." ~Albert Einstein

Whatever your understanding of the source of all that exists, be it from an organized faith, science, a fusion of these, or none of these, cultivating a relationship with the Source of your understanding can create a sense of peace, understanding, humility and awe. It can also be the most supportive of all the building blocks of our compassionate container.

When I give thanks in my daily practice, I give it to Source first. None of my practice or experience would be possible without the flame that sparks all creation. In recognizing the Source as that which it is, the origin of all being, I develop a direct understanding of my place within creation. And with that, a relationship with the ultimate companion.

When I'm faced with a difficult situation that my own skill set cannot navigate, I remind myself that I am not alone on this journey. That there is an energy, of which I'm only a part, that is swirling through the cosmos. I am just one flame combusting on the vast ball of fire that is the ultimate sun and if I hold on, and stay consciously connected to the Source, then the resulting flame will be effortless, graceful and most likely elegant.

Grasping this as fully as I can, I rest in the awareness that I am contained within the larger whole, though am co-creating with it. That I am not creating all of this, but I am contributing to it by who I am and how I show up. Showing up as the best me that I can be is the best thing to do for the whole unfolding. This is restful and encouraging to me, as I don't need to be anything other than the best me I can be.

Cultivating a relationship with the Source, in itself, can be an inspiring journey. This journey can include digging deep to our own cultural and religious history, exploring creation stories and traditions of other cultures and historical periods, delving into quantum physics, or cosmos theory.

Today, given our vast resources through technology to explore not only across cultures, but across time, we will most likely have an amalgam for our definition of Source to carry with us and guide us. Even if we choose an age old religious faith, those, too, arose from the intermingling of cultures and traditions.

Guided Reflections

 Do you have a direct relationship with the Source of your understanding?

 If not, the invitation in discovering a source to companion you on your sacred journey is to see how it resonates with you. Use the awareness exercises we're exploring as a touchstone to your defining--or not defining--the Source. What is the felt sense when you contemplate a particular idea of Source?

Most of us would like a Source that supports and cares for us. One that we can turn to in a time of unknowing that will give us guidance and reassurance for the next step on our path. What characteristics would you like to see in the Source?

 What relationship would you like to develop and foster with the Source?

Deities and Animal Companions

"In the beginning of all things, wisdom and knowledge were with the animals, for Tirawa, the One Above, did not speak directly to man. He sent certain animals to tell men that he showed himself through the beast, and that from them, and from the stars and the sun and moon should man learn...all things tell of Tirawa.." ~Eagle Chief (Letakos-Lesa) Pawnee

"There is nothing better that you can give to a person than to be present with them. When you are fully present, you become love, and you share that becoming with others." - attributed to Kuan Yin

Close to our relationship with the Source is the cultivating of relationships with certain characteristics and qualities that we may be wanting or needing in any given moment. Religious traditions such as Greek mythology, Hinduism, Buddhism, Christianity and many indigenous cultural practices personify these qualities in their deities.

For example, in Greek philosophy, Sophrosyne is seen as the Goddess of moderation and self-control. She is best summed up in the two phrases from the Oracle of Delphi, "Know thyself." and "Nothing in excess." I've found this goddess can be a valuable ally in my sacred journey, particularly when dealing with desires and cravings.

As well, First Peoples' traditions often look to the animal kingdom to demonstrate particular traits and characteristics.

The connection with the animal kingdom is strong in these cultures and some believe that each individual should have many animals as their guiding spirits. Though not always in physical relationship, some animal connections remain throughout life, some only for a particular time or circumstance. Needless to say, my journey with Shyla brought me closer to all in the animal kingdom.

Hawks and owls have been powerful animal guides in my adult life. A Native American spiritual elder, who is a sister to me on the path, once told me that owls were messengers--not necessarily of bad news, as I once believed, but just of news coming. I find myself, when seeing or hearing owls, perking up a bit and taking notice of my surroundings and life circumstances and try to stay a bit more aware in the coming time.

Living on the land at the cabin where silence created the opportunity to hear all the sounds of the creatures in my community, many nights were filled with owl sounds moving through the oak-forested hills. Barn owls, screeching owls and, my favorite, flammulated owls, would call from distances to each other. I felt it quite a treasure to be in the midst of their communications and nighttime movements.

It wasn't until the summer prior to my leaving the land that they actually revealed themselves to me. On two instances while walking up the path to the cabin, a small owl had positioned itself in a tree and called out. Even with my headlamp square on it, s/he afforded me a look at his/her white speckled feathers and big round face.

When I first moved off the land, owls greeted me at my new home, which helped me feel that I had made the right move. I

Compassion. In Mahayana Buddhism, a Bodhisattva is a being who is able to reach total enlightenment, but delays doing so out of compassion to save suffering and entangled beings on the path to enlightenment.

Quan Yin is seen in virtually every Asian culture and translates as "observing the sounds (or cries) of the world." She is seen as an effeminate male in early Chinese culture and is known in Sanskrit as Avaloketesvara, the Goddess of Mercy.

Compassion is the kind regard for a person's situation or circumstance. It is rooted in taking the time to listen and understand how a situation is affecting someone. Learning to be compassionate with ourselves is an absolutely necessary component of our spiritual journey. Equally, compassion for others has a tendency to arise naturally as we learn to cultivate it for ourselves. We can consciously and mindfully extend compassion to others.

Whether you choose to personify qualities and characteristics through deities, or just contemplate upon the characteristics themselves, I encourage you to become observant of qualities and characteristics you would like or need to cultivate for your journey.

Guided Reflections

 What animals or deities have you been attracted to throughout your life?

 What are their primary or subtle characteristics that attract, frighten or repel you?

Take note, as these deities and totems may be companioning you. It may be a skill or trait you share and admire, ones you need to learn, or something that you need to companion you at this point in your journey.

Using your journal to explore these characteristics, if it is an animal that attracts you, you may find it helpful to be with them, if possible, and observe them in their own habitat. Sketching, storytelling and photographing them can help foster your relationship. With other deities, having a physical representation can be a helpful reminder of the qualities and characteristics they represent.

Loving Kindness (Metta) Meditation

Learning to be kind and considerate towards ourselves and others is an important foundation for creating a compassionate container for our sacred journey. Most Buddhist meditation practices include a period of time devoted to generating loving kindness towards ourselves and others.

It is sometimes suggested that the focus of the loving kindness be towards oneself for the first 30 days of practice. After that, one can expand the circle to include loved ones, acquaintances, and people with whom we may have had or are having difficulties with. With more development of our practice, we can begin to include all the beings on the planet and beyond.

The practice is designed to be kept simple by repeating a few easy phrases over and again. (When you begin, pay particular attention to your responses, both emotional and physical, to the phrases. These can be clues as to areas where you may need to apply a little compassion towards yourself.)

Pick a few of the phrases that resonate best with you, or use these to develop your own:

May I be filled with loving kindness
May I be well in mind and body
May I be peaceful and ease in mind and body
May I experience much joy and happiness
May I be free from suffering
May I be happy
May I be free from illness and discomfort
May I have increasing causes for joy and happiness

Devote 10 minutes a day of generating loving kindness towards yourself for 30 days. Use your journal to reflect on your reactions to repeating the phrases. Take note over time how you feel after the exercise.

Faith as Companion

"Doubt is a pain too lonely to know that faith is his twin brother." ~Khalil Gibran

"None of us knows what might happen even the next minute, yet still we go forward. Because we trust. Because we have Faith." ~Paulo Coelho

"Faith is taking the first step even when you don't see the whole staircase." ~Martin Luther King, Jr.

"Faith is a knowledge within the heart, beyond the reach of proof." ~Khalil Gibran

Sometimes our path becomes muddied by circumstances and clarity is far at bay. When Shyla passed, there was a period of time that I had no sense of direction. Most of my choices towards the end of her life revolved around her care and path of decline. She was a central factor in the decisions I made, including where and how to live.

In the first months when she was gone, I had no sense of purpose. I recognized this as part of the mourning process--we had lived together for 15 years taking care of each others' needs. The depression was weighing heavy and I had to make extra concerted efforts to stay connected in my community of friends during this time.

I was fortunate in a sense because so much was going on at the time of her passing. I had begun a women's mindfulness meditation group, the house where we moved was in need of repairs, inspections and the like, and my consulting work for a local food co-op and other clients were keeping me busy.

But, there was just a flat, non-joyfulness around everything I did. Nothing made sense anymore and I couldn't see that I could ever experience joy again. While I knew these were signs of depression and mourning, it didn't change how I felt. I couldn't see what my next steps should be, except on a day to day basis. I had trouble making plans and working out timelines for necessary actions for the projects I was working on. I had never experienced this lack of clarity except when my mother died when I was in my early 30's.

Interestingly, an awareness arose one night when driving home from a gathering. The roads were wet from the warm rain that fell gently and there were pockets of fog on the windy mountain road. I suddenly saw how what was happening in my life right now was like driving through one of these pockets of fog. I couldn't see but maybe a few car lengths ahead, but given that I had driven the road many times and there were stretches of road I could see, I plunged forward on the faith that the road was there beyond what I could actually see in the pocket of fog. I had to trust that nothing had happened to the road.

I realized in that moment what it meant to have faith and that I could use this metaphor at this most difficult time in my life. When not being able to see that I had a purpose beyond being Shyla's caregiver and companion, I saw that I could trust--have faith--that there would be a road ahead for me.

I'm still not able to see the road far in front of me, but this faith and continuing to do what is before me at this moment is keeping me going. In recovery circles, they call this putting one foot in front of the other.

Guided reflections

 What does faith mean to you?

 What do you have faith in?

 If you are not sure you have faith in anything, other than what you can see, think about what happens for you when you turn on a light switch. Do you have faith that it will turn on, even though you can't see the wires and electricity behind the switch?

Addiction and Recovery

"I have absolutely no pleasure in the stimulants in which I sometimes so madly indulge. It has not been in the pursuit of pleasure that I have periled life and reputation and reason. It has been the desperate attempt to escape from torturing memories, from a sense of insupportable loneliness and a dread of some strange impending doom." ~Edgar Allan Poe

"The true way to be humble is not to stoop until you're lower than yourself but to stand at your real height against some higher nature that will show you the smallness of your greatness." ~Stephanie S. Covington, Ph.D.

Painful addiction is rampant in our culture. Addictions can be a dependency on those things that we may have heard of, drugs (pot, meth, psychedelics, prescription medicines, etc.) and alcohol, but they can also include an unhealthy dependency on food, relationships, debting, gambling, overeating, sex, shopping, love, TV, tobacco, caffeine, work and even exercise. (There are even people that are addicted to enabling addicts!)

Addictions are sometimes elusive and hard to define, especially when it is with things that we need to survive, such as food or love. Our culture, though, is saturated with the effects of multi-generational addiction. In addition to the addicted person, those with who they are in a relationship with can be adversely affected because an addiction eventually takes over other healthy and important things to the addict, including meaningful relationships.

Finding a way out of addiction can be quite challenging, especially when the substance is something that we need (food, love, work, shopping), and even more so when these substances are seen in the culture as providing pleasure (gambling, shopping, sex, etc.). Some addicts live lonely and painful lives hiding their addictions and some even die from them.

A big part of the problem for addicts finding a way out is that over time an addiction leads one into isolation--reaching out for help is the very hardest thing to do, but it is the most needed. It is usually not until the addict has created so much wreckage in their life through lost relationships, run-ins with the law, or severe illness that they seek help. In recovery circles, they call this "hitting bottom."

Today, there are many avenues to find help from addiction and most likely one just around the corner from where you live. Be they treatment centers, 12-Step meetings, psycho-social therapists, or reading materials, we have a wealth of information available to help us determine if we are, or know someone who is, caught in an addiction and where we can find help to relieve our pain and suffering.

For me, it took the end of a relationship, deep debt, homelessness and the innocent and well intentioned effort of a family member to enlighten me of my patterns of co-dependency and addiction. A simple book, "Co-dependent No More," by Melody Beatty simultaneously made me angry while giving me hope and a sense of relief. As at the age of almost 40 I read my life in the pages of this book, years of patterns leaped into my consciousness.

I was jaw-dropping dumbfounded that I could have lived these unhealthy and unsatisfying patterns for so long and not understood their source. I have heard similar reactions from many of my friends in recovery--how could they have lived so long in a pattern that was destroying their lives, bodies, minds and those they loved? The answer: Because that is the insidious nature of addiction.

But there is hope. There is so much hope! For me, being on a conscious spiritual path helped my healing process dramatically. For millions of others, too, the key lies in a spiritual foundation becoming THE top priority in life.

Much work on Codependence and Adult Children of Alcoholics issues has resulted in a graceful relief of the self- and other-induced pain and suffering that alcohol brought into my life. Healing childhood trauma, taking responsibility for my well being, life and choices, and healing relationships where my addictive patterns wreaked havoc has brought a new freedom and authenticity in my life. And a gratitude that I have a life worth living, when before I didn't.

Twelve-step programs are grounded in using a conscious spiritual path to relieve suffering. The idea is to build a relationship with a "Power Greater Than Myself" and allow this relationship to take precedence above all else. These programs approach the "Power" as something that can only be determined and defined by the addict seeking relief, so there is no pressure to adopt a particular definition or religious faith.

Many 12-step meetings take place within the walls of churches and the foundations of the first 12-step program, Alcoholics Anonymous, was founded by Christian men. During the evolution of Alcoholics Anonymous, it became quite clear that the God that was referred to in their teachings had to be defined by the person suffering from addiction for the program to be successful.

Some of the healing work that I attended to when first coming into recovery was my Catholic upbringing. The strict father-figure story of creation that Catholicism is based upon helped create my patterns of unworthiness and low self-esteem.

Today, though, I can see how this religion also sparked in me an affinity for ritual, quiet contemplation, and a recognition that there is a divineness in all that is and in all of us. Having done the healing work, my Catholic roots can now be incorporated and expressed in a way that is healthy and divine for me.

My compulsions and addictive patterns will show themselves when I deviate from my spiritual foundations of meditation, contemplation and connection with nature. It is a good indicator for me when I'm out of balance in my life. Thanks to the tools of recovery, I have the means to get back on track when this happens.

Guided reflections

 Do you feel that you are living an unhealthy pattern or indulging in a substance that you can't seem to stop?

 Are you closely involved with someone that seems to have an addiction towards a pattern or substance?

If so, take some time and explore the characteristics associated with that possibly addictive pattern/substance. Sometimes, just the awareness that this pattern exists can help make a shift, but also know there are many avenues for addressing these issues and a vibrant, healthy and free life awaits on the other side. The internet has information and quizzes on all addictive patterns and groups to help find a solution.

Also, if so, over time, as your compassionate container and practice grow, what do you notice about these patterns? For me, they allowed the core issues behind these patterns to bubble to the surface to be looked at, healed and released. Your journal and practice can prove to be a valuable friend as you look at these patterns over time.

Grace as Companion

Grace is that divinely elegant moment or situation that shouldn't be, but is, and attributed by no cause of our own, save being there.

Resting in the Buddha nature, the rest unfolds.

Including grace as companion seems most appropriate when I reflect on how I moved, or I should say, was moved, into my current home. Grace has happened so many times in my life, but this was the most recent and poignant.

I had been looking for a home for over one and half years. I had qualified for loans, unqualified for loans; qualified for a first time home buyers program; unqualified for a first time home buyers program. I had submitted multiple offers on homes that would have sufficed for my move off the hill only to be declined for one reason or another. These homes weren't ideal, but I was moving from a single-room 256 square foot cabin-- my expectations were not high, nor were my needs.

I watched house after house get bought and moved into by people that weren't me. I had envisioned what I liked and wanted and what I didn't like and didn't want in a home. Shyla and I traveled all over the area looking for our new home. The basic requirements were easy access for our aging bodies in a small and affordable place.

When the second September of looking for a new home came, I felt an energy begin to move me down the hill from the cabin. There was nothing on the horizon for purchase, but I knew that I didn't want to spend another winter in the cabin and that I didn't want to move all my belongings down the hill, by wheelbarrow, in the rains. So I began the move and it seemed effortless.

An energy swept over me and within a week, most of my belongings acquired over the past ten years were transported down the hill and stored on a pallet under a tarp. I had no idea where I was going, but the energetic sense was clear--I was moving.

Shyla's health at the time was relatively good. She stayed and rested at the cabin as I made multiple trips with an overstuffed rickety wheelbarrow swaying and swerving down the hill. It was one of the most clear, but bizarre times for me. I knew I was moving--but where?

I arranged with both a friend and my intimate partner to look at a rental house in the area I wanted to live. As I was driving to meet them at the local coffee house, which is just across the street from my realtor's office, I received a call from my realtor. I was literally driving past his office.

He said he had a possible house for me. It would be a short sale. I told him I would be glad to see it after we looked at the rental. As with each of the places I had looked at previously, the rental would have worked, though it didn't have the best access for Shyla and it was on a hillside, which would make it difficult for us to take walks.

When I pulled up and saw the carport and single step entry to the house my realtor showed us, I knew almost in an instant that this house would meet our needs. But as we entered the doorway and the old polished wood floors and light wood trim on the doors and windows greeted me, I became humbled. This was far more than I had hoped for.

There were still leftover belongings from the owners and some fundamental things, like a monitor heater, stove and the toilet (!) had been stolen, but Shyla and I felt at home instantly and within a few days, contracts to rent and to purchase this magnificent house had been signed. Without missing a step, we were moved in within two weeks.

The beauty and the grace of the neighborhood humbled me as we watched the fall color parade. I was now living in an area like those where Shyla and I used to drive long distances to spend our vacations. Tall pines, cedars, maples and even dogwood trees lined the narrow streets high in the mountains. Little vacation cabins dotted the neighborhood and there was a quiet like that which can only be found in deep woods.

The grace? This home was far more than I had hoped for at a time that became critical in Shyla's life. I could not have bought this house prior, because the conventional financing I qualified for, then no longer qualified for, wouldn't allow a non-municipal water source and this home is sourced at a spring. A spring! I didn't even have that possibility on my list! I had been drinking spring water for the past 25 years and bathing in rain water for the past 10. It didn't even occur to me that I could be graced with piped in running spring water. This was the real icing on the cake!

We had moved into the house in time to allow Shyla her last month or so of life to be spent in ease and comfort. Regardless of whether I was able to purchase the house became irrelevant. The fact that we could have it together for her final days was all that was important.

As I wend my way through the closing process, which has taken over 6 months now, I continue to focus my attention on my spiritual path and cultivating my "Buddha-nature," because I know that then, the rest unfolds--grace happens in its most elegant and unfettered nature--and in spite of myself sometimes. Even with all my "trying to make things happen," grace finds its way into my life again and again.

But, grace is not something that can be anticipated or forced. It seems to only arise out of circumstances that are beyond my control and I only seem to fully recognize it after the fact. It seems to happen when I've let go of something completely. Each time, I'm humbled to know that there is something operating so inconceivably elegant and beautiful that I am taken aback and jaw-dropped-in-awe each time it occurs.

The profundity is not only in that exquisite things occur, but the circumstances leading up to them are sometimes seemingly chaotic and unrelated, and yet, somehow, voila! Magnificence happens.

Guided Reflections

 Have you had times when circumstances or a situation happened when you thought, "Wow! That should NOT have happened that way!" Write about them in your journal.

 What do you think is the source of these graceful acts?

Gratitude as Companion

"Experiencing and expressing gratitude is an important part of any spiritual practice. It opens the heart and activates positive emotion centers in the brain. Regular practice of gratitude can change the way our brain neurons fire into more positive automatic patterns. The positive emotions we evoke can soothe distress and broaden our thinking patterns so we develop a larger and more expansive view of our lives. Gratitude is an emotion of connectedness, which reminds us we are part of a larger universe with all living things."
~Melanie Greenberg, Ph.D.

"Trade your expectation for appreciation and your world changes instantly." ~Tony Robbins

"If the only prayer you said in your whole life was 'thank you,' that would suffice." ~Meister Eckhart

When I think back on all the experiences and circumstances that have created my life today, I can have nothing but gratitude. All the patterns, people and choices that have landed me here were not necessarily the most conscious or loving, but they brought me to this moment--this unrepeatable, irreplaceable moment. For that I am grateful.

I have worked with gratitude mostly in my practice with affirmations and when I first started working with them in recovery, their impact was profound.

When my practice included jotting down three things that I was grateful for each evening for a month, my world became astonishingly full, even though I had very few physical possessions. My circumstances from someone looking in would have been considered sparse at best, and most would have had pity on me.

It was at the time I was living in the cabin. A single room (16x16ft) with a loft and no running water, no indoor plumbing, a couple of solar panels for lighting, and an eighth of a mile hike up the oak-forested hills of Lake County on a deer trail. My only heat source was an old cracked inefficient wood stove and I had to carry every stick of wood I burned up a steep grade, since the cabin was perched on a knoll.

I sometimes hiked up to one quarter of a mile with a backpack full of wood that I had cut somewhere on the land with a chainsaw and split with a maul. I hauled five gallon tanks of propane up the hill for cooking, hauled all drinking and cooking water and I showered with two gallons of water using a cup.

Hearing this, one may think that I lived a poor, hard existence and I can honestly say that I wouldn't have chosen this lifestyle prior to having lived it. Circumstances landed me there, but when circumstances changed and I had the means to live differently, I stayed for another seven years! It was how my circumstances changed from no real choice to one of living in voluntary simplicity.

It was during this period that my practice included a month of reflecting on at least three things I was grateful for each day. It was so easy to find a whole host of things to be grateful for, but it usually boiled down to the same three: Shyla, my home, and being in a relationship with someone that was emotionally present with me.

I like to spend conscious time in gratitude and I like to work with my clients in this arena. It can sometimes be hard to notice things in our own lives, or current situations to be grateful for-- especially if we are being challenged by difficult circumstances. Focusing on gratitude can help companion us through difficult times or when our minds can only see the negative side of our situation. It is a source of inspiration and, as Melody Beatty says, it can turn what we have into more.

Guided Reflections

 Just off the top of your head, how many things can you jot down in your journal that you are grateful for?

 Designate a portion of your daily journal writing to keeping a gratitude list for 30 days. In that time, make note of your thoughts and feelings about the exercise. When you are finished, look back at your beginning thoughts and compare them with the thoughts towards the end of the 30-days. What do you notice about your shift in perspective and attitude with gratitude?

IV

Companioning with Others

"The path to love begins in our own past and its healing, then moves outward to relationships with others." ~David Richo, How to be an Adult in Relationship

"Life gives us brief moments with another...but sometimes in those brief moment we get memories that last a life time..." ~Unknown

Because we are dialogical beings, all of our life takes place in relationship. Whether with ourself, others, our environment, community or planet, how we relate to these various "others" can immensely affect our journey. As well, who we relate to and what role they play in our lives will contribute to the nature of our journey.

We'll take a brief journey into beginning relationships with our family of origin and then take a look at our romantic relationships and relationships with those in our spiritual community.

Family of Origin

"You don't choose your family. They are God's gift to you, as you are to them." ~Desmond Tutu

Our family of origin provides our first opportunity for discovering who we are in relation to others. It is also the place where much pain and anguish can arise as we go through the process of self-discovery.

If, as in many cases, one is blessed to have their basic physical, emotional and spiritual needs met, they have a good chance of learning how to be a healthy and loving self and can move into relationships with others in a balanced and nurturing way that provides growth, optimism, self-discovery and a continued flourishing of expanded capabilities and capacity.

If, on the other hand, one's family of origin falls short in the basic needs of love, respect, security and support, then we may begin to actively seek these from all of our other relationships. If we don't have these mirrored to us when young, it can be a struggle to find these in others and ourselves, as we don't have the model to know what we are seeking. We just know we are in need and our need isn't being met. We also begin looking at the models in the larger culture to mimic and sometimes adopt characteristics we admire or think are important.

When we are young, and our basic needs have not been met, we can also find ourselves looking to fantasy and fairytales as an idea of what love and caring is supposed to look like. Indeed, our American culture is rife with these images.

As youths, we may not understand that these are categorized as fantasy and fairytales because they are unattainable, so we may begin seeking these ideal characteristics in ourselves and relationships with others. We will most likely be disappointed time and again when we and others fall short. This can sometimes create a painful cycle of hope, disappointment and self-deprecation.

How do we take care of ourselves at our current stage in life if we were not met with the basic needs of love, respect, security and support? Since we can't control the past (in essence the container that we were raised in), the healing work begins with us and our willingness to meet ourselves with a kind, caring and compassionate attention. This undertaking is an act of love and support for ourselves and can create a tremendous healing opportunity.

For me, the process of learning how to take care of and love myself in a healthy way began in adulthood. I had to basically re-parent myself. I thought back at what traits I really wished I had seen in, and experienced from, my parents. I began a process of learning these qualities and re-parenting myself in a way that I had wanted to be met as a child: with patience, kindness, understanding, calmness, unconditional love, pampering, discipline, acceptance, attention and appreciation.

I (like my parents) was not perfect at this, but over time, I've been able to incorporate most of these traits for how I work with and treat myself. The self-deprecating talk and behaviors began to stop. And now, when I hear those old tapes, I can most times dismiss them immediately.

When my own reparenting took hold, all my relationships evolved because I was no longer looking for others to meet my basic needs. I met myself. I grew into a mostly healthy and balanced human being that can get most of my basic needs met most of the time. And the times I can't, I have the patience and understanding to companion myself through the disappointment.

We may not have had the fortunate opportunity to be raised with our basic needs for love, security, safety and health met and we may have adopted some unhealthy emotional and physical patterns, but we can learn how to meet ourselves with the loving kindness all humanity deserves.

It is a growth process and one that can carry a sweet essence as we meet ourselves with the tenderness and caring we most enjoy. It can also be a delightful path of self-discovery.

Guided Reflections

 What traits, qualities and characteristics of your family of origin do you most admire and want to carry on?

 What are some behaviors you would prefer not to carry on?

 If you had the perfect parent, how would that parent treat you? Is this how you treat yourself? If not, consider incorporating one or two of the desired characteristics or behaviors towards your self-care.

Intimate Relationships

"We come to love not by finding a perfect person, but by learning to see an imperfect person perfectly." ~Sam Keen

The partners we choose in life usually reflect our self understanding at the time and can create tremendous opportunities for growth. Is it any wonder that there are literally millions of books written on the subject of intimate relationship? I'm addressing intimate relationships in a brief and limited way in hopes of opening the reader to how we form relationships and how they affect our spiritual path.

I had spent most of my adult life looking for a partner similar to those depicted in the traditional stories of my youth--a Prince Charming that was handsome and met all of my needs and desires.

In my relationships, if the person I was with did not meet these criteria, within a few years I would be looking for ways to help them become this person for me, whether they wanted to or not. Little did I know I was acting on some very deep unconscious programming.

Over time, I would become quite manipulative and this pattern would result in much pain for myself, not having my needs met, and for my partner, as they could never live up to this image. They were left feeling inadequate, judged and wrong.

As my spiritual path strengthened and I began to understand the misconceptions about relationship that had been perpetrated through popular media and cultural story, I came to see how I wrongly held others to a standard that was not only not possible, but could never really have created any deep and lasting meaning for me in relationship.

There are many helpful relationship books and theories available today (some listed in the resource section in the back) that have helped guide me to the understandings I hold to be true and valuable today.

There is a common thread through each of these books that have touched me--from the classics by Rumi and Kahlil Gibran through contemporaries like David Richo. That thread is a self awareness and self understanding so deep and true that we are better able to communicate our needs and desires clearly with our partner.

The thread also includes the letting go of needing our partner to meet all of our needs--which puts them in the awkward position of potentially becoming our Higher Power. Richo believes that we should only look to receive 25% of our nurturance from a healthy intimate relationship. The rest, we find within ourselves.

On a particular morning when my intimate partner and I were conversing about marriage, this pattern in my relationship history became quite apparent. I was again going to see my partner as someone wrong for me and then make it about him.

The beauty of this particular relationship was that we had done the work early on to create a safe enough container to have any conversation without jeopardizing the relationship. We both knew that we could be triggered by situations that would call us to look at our past, but we also knew we were safe to explore these triggers with each other. This gave us the opportunity to heal past harms and misunderstandings from way back in our family of origin or other romantic relationships, as well as learn to accept and respect our differences as we moved forward in our relationship.

The sacredness of this container that we had worked to create was a powerful companion for even deeper healing from situations that could not have come to the forefront without being in relationship. This relationship in particular really helped me shift my understanding about what characteristics were truly important and necessary for me for an intimate partner. It also helped me see that my needs were not about my partner's failings. My intimate partners were not wrong in who they were and what they wanted and needed. This was a profound revelation in my relationship pattern!

I've learned that for my highest good for creating my compassionate container, the person with whom I'm involved needs to be emotionally present enough with themselves to be emotionally present with me. They also need to have a willingness to create a safe container to experience the ups and downs of the relationship and the triggers, as well as a self-understanding and independence that leaves me room to be on my own. (This holds true for my platonic relationships as well.)

With this capacity, my relationships can become a sacred companion on my journey. One that allows me to heal my psyche, deepen my presencing skills and provides for a joyful and sometimes ecstatic union.

Pursuing my own spiritual path is vitally important for the success of my relationships--intimate or platonic. When our own container and practice is strong, we find most of our needs met in the relationship with ourselves and the divine. This leaves the relationships with our friends and intimate partners to be ones of caring, concern, mutual respect, joyful union and sometimes a safe place to work out patterns of past relationships.

Guided Reflections

 What would you need in your intimate relationship to feel you had a safe container? Emotional availability? Commitment? Honesty? Respectful and kind communication?

 Have you noticed any patterns that you live in your intimate relationships that may not be healthy? What would you change about those patterns? Do you play a roll in perpetuating the pattern? Is there another way for you to respond?

Community (Sangha)

"If in our daily life we can smile, if we can be peaceful and happy, not only we, but everyone will profit from it. This is the most basic kind of peace work." ~Thich Nhat Hanh

"Some people think they are in community, but they are only in proximity. True community requires commitment and openness. It is a willingness to extend yourself to encounter and know the other." ~David Spangler

"I alone cannot change the world, but I can cast a stone across the waters to create many ripples." ~Mother Teresa

Bringing our practice out beyond our one-on-one relationships is touching our world with who we are. We sometimes do this in community, or *Sangha*. Sangha is Sanskrit for community or association. It can be as simple as a small group of women meeting once a month to discuss their discoveries, joys, sorrows and pain; a group that you experience a particular event with that touches you deeply; or an ongoing group of practitioners that meet in a formal setting with a standard set of practices shared, such as that with a group of monks or nuns that practice together.

You could belong to many different sanghas that create an ever-increasing set of petals on a flower of which you are the center. Likewise, each of those who belong to your various sanghas, through their different connections, is the center of their flowers. This vision can create a beautiful conceptual understanding of the flower of life and the interconnectedness of us all.

I've had unbelievable phenomenal experiences with people I hadn't previously known through chance encounters at public events, meeting out in nature and even standing in line at the store. When an attitude of "we're all in this together" begins to pervade one's perspective, every experience becomes one to share with those on the path--and we're all on the path to awakening, even if it isn't the same path, or a conscious one. When we can see this and begin tending to each other with kindness and caring, everyone becomes our sangha.

On a more personal and individual level, something about the ongoing support of a group of individuals that come together for a common purpose creates a net of security and safety with which to have an experience. It also increases the power and deepens the effect of the individuals involved, as the whole is always greater than the sum of the parts.

I started a women's meditation group in my community recently. We chose to use mindfulness meditation as the basis for our work together. Instantly, the strength in my meditation deepened when I was in the presence of the group, much like happens when I'm on extended retreat with a large group of practitioners.

On extended retreat, a group of individuals come together for a period of time and consciously create a sangha of support. We make agreements to remain in silence during the retreat; to not disturb or intrude on another's silence unless absolutely necessary; and to abide by the five precepts (Buddhist code of conduct) of restraint from harming, taking anything that isn't ours, sexual misconduct, lying and intoxication.

These agreements, along with others, create the container for our practice together during the retreat; they help create the conditions for self-realization. It is a beautiful thing when we come together with intention to support ourselves and each other in this way. The profundity of this usually hits me at some point on the retreat and I am moved to tears of awe and gratitude that a group of strangers would do this for me--for my practice, my awakening.

Companioning in this way provides a unique opportunity for fellowship that extends beyond our known circle of friends and takes it to a new level of community--with our fellow humans.

On a more local and personal level, in our meditation group not all women can make it each time, but there are enough of us flowing in and out to create a net of like-minded practitioners to maintain the benefits of sangha. On an ongoing basis, belonging to one or more sanghas, whether it be for a spiritual practice, or another common endeavor, can bring a spirit of companionship that strengthens our practice, friendships and understanding what it is to be supportive and in community.

The benefits of our spiritual practice, as well, have a ripple effect on our communities at large--whether at work, play or in education. Who we are and how we show up affects the outcomes of situations. Bringing our highest intentions and full attention increases the chances for more heartfelt and meaningful experiences.

Guided Reflections

 Do you have a group that you belong to that can be considered a sangha? What do you gain from this group beyond the intended reason for gathering?

 If you don't belong to a group, what area of your practice would you like to connect with one? Writing? Sitting meditation? Walking? Exercise? Something else?

 In seeking a sangha, what would be the conditions of the container you would like to see?

V

Companioning the Final Journey

"Watching a peaceful death of a human being reminds us of a falling star; one of a million lights in a vast sky that flares up for a brief moment only to disappear into the endless night forever."
~Elisabeth Kubler-Ross

"Ever has it been that love knows not its own depth until the hour of separation." ~ Kahlil Gibran

Those final moments of wakefulness with ourselves and others give us the crux of Buddhist teachings-- it is indeed temporary and we are impermanent.

When Shyla's health began to fail, I knew it was time to make a move. As I mentioned earlier, we had been living remotely for over ten years together and she was fourteen, which is quite old for a large Shepherd mix. Our chop wood, carry water lifestyle was a blessing in so many ways, but it dawned on me one day as I pushed the wheelbarrow full of our day's shopping up the hill, that there may come a time when Shyla wouldn't be able to make the eighth mile journey up the sweeping slopes to the cabin.

I had already needed to get help for my wood gathering for the past few winters, so my days of being able to live like this were numbered as well. Our search for a new home began in the summer of 2011 and, as I mentioned previously, my prayer became, "Thank you for my good friend Shyla. Thank you for guiding me in how to best care for and love her as she finds her way to You."

That prayer began a deep and meaningful path of transition for Shyla that helped me companion her to her final breath in the Winter of 2012 in the bedroom in our new home. We had searched for over a year and half for our new home and for reasons beyond comprehension, we landed in a dwelling that far exceeded my hopes and desires.

Shyla had a stroke that left her dizzy and unable to walk straight. Within a week, she had seemingly fully recovered and our life continued. Within another week, she had another stroke that rendered her unable to walk on her own. This signaled the final few days of her life and triggered my natural instinct to care for her tenderly while reading up on the Buddhist traditions for the dying.

Shyla and I had helped care for my father and were present for his passing some ten years prior. She had an innate sense of his passing as we lay next to his bed while he took his last breaths. I knew that I would be doing the same for Shyla, both as her companion in life and companion on the spiritual path.

The next days were filled with setting up an altar close by her; consulting with my dear friends, one of which was her veterinarian; tending to her bodily needs; and prayer and meditation according to the Buddhist practices. I spent many hours next to her doing Metta (loving kindness) meditation for her.

My emotions oscillated between companioning her final spiritual journey and experiencing the loss of my best friend. It was one of the most challenging things I've had to do. In the end, when I knew it was close, I had to decide whether to meditate or lay with her and hold her. My partner had lain with her through most of the night while I meditated, but he needed to go to bed. Torn, I let the meditation go because I couldn't imagine her passing without being held and touched by me.

As I lay next to her, her breath began to change into a rote repetition that was almost machine like. I knew we were close. The minutes passed and her breath began to slow down. I stroked her gently not wanting to disturb anything, but still wanting to hold space with her.

As her breath wound down, I kissed her on her forehead, as I had done a million times before. In that instant, her body jerked up and away from me like it was being pulled, or she was pulling away from me. This startled me and I pulled back as she lay back down. It was her last breath.

The tears flowed instantly, not out of loss of my friend, but out of the incredulous understanding of what I just witnessed and experienced. The past 14 years of my life were a gift of this incredible being's life--the joy, the love, the wisdom and understanding, the gamut of our experiences. But, in her final days, I received the gift of being consciously present with her for her passing. She gifted me her life--and now her death.

I laid with her for many hours and cleaned her body and prepared it according to scripture. I laid with her until it was clear in my body that she was gone and I was no longer with Shyla, but with a corpse that lay lifeless.

In some traditions it is believed that the 72 hours following death is the period of time it takes for the soul to leave the body. In honoring these traditions, I experienced the decay of her body over the next few days before taking it to the crematorium. In certain Buddhist traditions, it is common for monks to practice meditation in charnel grounds, so as to become acutely aware of the temporariness of the body. I used this opportunity to deepen my practice as well as honor my lost friend.

There was a heightened sense of awareness and wakefulness during this period that is unexplainable. I can say that directly experiencing Shyla's death was one of the most profound and important experiences of my life, as was being present for my mother's and father's last breaths.

It makes me wonder if it is the same as attending a birth, since I have neither given birth nor attended one. I believe, though, that they both are portal times of significance. Equal? It's hard to say from this end--that of which loses the being. In any case, creating a mindful and dignified container of compassion, whether it is for another's or our own death, seems to me to be one of the most gracious and giving things we can do on our journey.

I recently read a piece that was written from the perspective of a fetus on the eve of its birth and how all the significant signs and events that we would see as indications of the birth coming, it was seeing as its death--leaving the amniotic sac and the warmth of inside the womb and having to begin breathing air and feeding through a mouth--these were all signs of the end of its life as it knew it. Much like that with the life cycle of a caterpillar--it may seem like the end, but it may be just the beginning of a transformative awakening.

Guided Reflections

 Have you attended another's death? What was your experience?

 How would you like to spend your last moments? Who would you like to be there?

VI

The Sacred Journey Onward

"Courage doesn't mean you don't get afraid. Courage means you don't let fear stop you."~ Bethany Hamilton

"Your daily life is your temple and your religion. When you enter into it take with you your all." ~Kahlil Gibran

"It is not given to us to know how our life will affect the world. What is given to us is to tend the intentions of our heart and to plant beautiful seeds with our deeds. Do not doubt that your good actions will bear fruit, and that change for the better can be born from your life." ~Jack Kornfield

We've voyaged together learning how to companion ourselves and others on a sacred journey. Undertaking this path is a vital and worthy step in a life worth living--a life of authenticity and profundity.

The tools presented here are really only the beginning of a beautiful and sturdy sacred container. But, if your journey is undertaken with a genuine and open heart, these tools will lead you to the right next turn on the adventurous path.

Follow your intuition at every turn, even if it is seemingly wrong on occasion. It is said by many that there are no mistakes on this journey.

I wish you the kindest regards on your path and in creating your compassionate container. We do not know what our future holds, though we can take steps to help mold it; we can set a course and contribute to the outcome. Along the way we will most likely touch and be touched by many.

May your growing consciousness and practice benefit all sentient beings.

~Awakened Presence of the Heart

www.companioningthesacredjourney.com

_____

Further Reading

Allen, James, (1902). As a Man Thinketh. (1963 edition) London: Collins.

Browne Walker, Brian. (1992). The I Ching or Book of Changes: A Guide to Life's Turning Points. NY: St. Martin's Griffin.

Carnes, Robin Deen & Craig, Sally. (1998). Sacred Circles: A Guide to Creating Your Own Women's Spirituality Group. San Francisco: HarperSanFrancisco.

Chopra, Deepak. (1994). The Seven Spiritual Laws of Success: A Practical Guide to the Fulfillment of Your Dreams. San Rafael, CA: Amber-Allen Publishing & New World Library.

Cohen, Alan. (1996). A Deep Breath of Life: Daily Inspiration for Heart-Centered Living. Carlsbad, CA: Hay House, Inc.

Covington, Ph.D., Stephanie S. (1994). A Woman's Way Through the Twelve Steps. Center City, MN: Hazelden.

Gibran, Kahlil. (1927). The Prophet. New York: Alfred A Knopf.

Hay, Louise. (1984). You Can Heal Your Life. Hay House, Inc.

Kornfield, Jack. (2008). A Path With Heart: The Classic Guide Through The Perils And Promises Of Spiritual Life. New York: Bantam Books.

Lama, H.H. Dalai & Cutler, Howard C. (2009). The Art of Happiness, Tenth Anniversary Edition: A Handbook for Living. New York: Riverhead Books.

Moore, Thomas. (1992). Care of the Soul: A Guide to Cultivating Depth and Sacredness in Everyday Life. New York: Harper-Collins Publishers, Inc.

Richo, David. (2006). The Five Things We Cannot Change: And the Happiness We Find by Embracing Them. Boston & London: Shambhala.

Richo, David. (2002). How to be an Adult in Relationships: The Five Keys to Mindful Loving. Boston & London: Shambhala.

Tsu, Lao. Tao Te Ching. (2012). Translated by Gia-fu Feng and Jane English. Forward by Jacob Needleman. NY: Vintage Books.

About the Author

JoAnn Saccato, MA received her Masters in Co-creating Sustainable Futures, a self-designed interdisciplinary program from Sonoma State University in 2009. She is a Reiki Master/ Teacher, inspirational speaker, educator, author and consultant living in the hills in Northern California. During her "chop wood, carry water" years at a remotely located cabin, she journeyed through recovery for codependency, completed her Bachelors and Masters degree, embarked on a spiritual pilgrimage to India to explore the sacred places of Sikhism, Hinduism and Buddhism, and helped found the Lake County Community Co-op.

JoAnn received her Dharma name, *Awakened Presence of the Heart,* while receiving the Three Jewels and Five Mindfulness Trainings in the Thich Nhat Hanh lineage at Camp Latize in 2007. She is available for speaking engagements, individual companioning sessions, meditation instruction, and Reiki healing and empowerments. For more information visit www.companioningthesacredjourney.com

Made in the USA
Middletown, DE
27 May 2015